BEETHOVEN

His Spiritual Development

BEETHOVEN

His
Spiritual Development

BY

J. W. N. SULLIVAN

VINTAGE BOOKS
A DIVISION OF RANDOM HOUSE
New York

VINTAGE BOOKS

are published by ALFRED A. KNOPF, INC.

and RANDOM HOUSE, INC.

Preface

BEETHOVEN's *music may be studied from many different aspects, but in this book I am concerned with one aspect only. From the technical point of view Beethoven's music can still yield rich finds to properly qualified searchers, as some of Dr. Tovey's magnificent essays abundantly prove. Also, Beethoven's influence on other composers is a study on which the last word has by no means been said. Again, Beethoven's music may be used to throw light on certain of his characteristics, his amazing constructive power, his dramatic sense, his humour, his impulsiveness, etc. etc. But in this book I am not primarily concerned with any of these aspects of his work. I am concerned with Beethoven's music solely as a record of his spiritual development. I believe that in his greatest music Beethoven was primarily concerned to express his personal vision of life. This vision was, of course, the product of his character and his experience. Beethoven the man and Beethoven the composer are not two unconnected entities, and the known history of* the man may be used to throw light upon the character of his music. This does not mean, of course, that successive compositions reflect successive incidents in his life. The life-work of a great artist is not some kind of sumptuous diary. But Beethoven's attitude towards life was largely conditioned by certain root experiences. Such experiences do not happen once for all. They have a life of their own, and they continue to modify the man's whole attitude towards life. They become combined with other experiences and form elements in continually more complex synthetic wholes. The development and transformation of Beethoven's attitude towards life, the result of certain root experiences can, I believe, be traced in his music. As the assumptions underlying this point of view conflict with ideas on the nature of music still held in some responsible quarters, I have devoted a preliminary section to a discussion of the general question.

For such biographical details as I have used in this work I am chiefly indebted to Mr. Krehbiel's edition of Thayer's Life of Beethoven. The interpretations given to the compositions I discuss are my own, but I have been much gratified to find that certain other writers have expressed similar ideas. Even when the ideas are worded very differently, it can be seen that the same fundamental experience of the composition is being expressed. No such interpretations can claim universal validity. The utmost they can do is to suggest to the reader that the author's experience of the composition is similar to his own. Such additional coherence and systematization as the author has given to his ideas may then be found profitable.

Beethoven's music, much more than that of any other

composer, inevitably prompts the kind of reflections that are contained in this book. Thus Mr. Ernest Newman has said, "It is the peculiarity of Beethoven's imagination that again and again he lifts us to a height from which we revaluate not only all music but all life, all emotion, and all thought." This "peculiarity" has long been recognized as the function of the greatest literature. It is also, we may believe, the function of the greatest music, although it performs that function in a very different way, and even if Beethoven's music be the only music sufficiently powerful to exercise it unambiguously.

J. W. N. SULLIVAN

Chobham, 1927

Contents

The Nature of Music

CHAPTER ONE

Art and Reality

ON MAY 28, 1810, Elizabeth Brentano, a young woman who is described as having been beautiful, highly cultured and fascinating, wrote a letter to Goethe describing her meeting with Beethoven. In the course of this letter she professes to report a conversation with Beethoven and attributes to him the following remarks:—

> "When I open my eyes I must sigh, for what I see is contrary to my religion, and I must despise the world which does not know that music is a higher revelation than all wisdom and philosophy, the wine which inspires one to new generative processes, and I am the Bacchus who presses out this glorious wine for mankind and makes them spiritually drunken. When they are again become sober they have drawn from the sea all that they brought with them, all that they can bring with them to dry land. I have not a single friend, I must

3

live alone. But well I know that God is nearer to me than to other artists; I associate with Him without fear; I have always recognized and understood Him and have no fear for my music—it can meet no evil fate. Those who understand it must be freed by it from all the miseries which the others drag about with themselves."

"Music, verily, is the mediator between intellectual and sensuous life."

"Speak to Goethe about me. Tell him to hear my symphonies and he will say that I am right in saying that music is the one incorporeal entrance into the higher world of knowledge which comprehends mankind but which mankind cannot comprehend."

On the following day, when Elizabeth showed Beethoven what she had written he exclaimed, "Did I say that? Well, then I had a raptus!"

But the question is whether Beethoven said any of it at all. It is an unfortunate fact that the fascinating Elizabeth was not a perfectly truthful person. Even her champion, Thayer, admits that she was not above forging documents, or parts of documents. And the remarks attributed to Beethoven in this letter certainly differ in style from anything to be found in his writings. Schindler, the constant associate of Beethoven in his last years, stated that he had never heard "the master" talk like it. On the other hand, Beethoven was at this time only forty years of age; he had not yet entered into the silence of his last years. And Elizabeth was indisputably far more intelligent and responsive than Schindler. Moreover there are certain points about the report which, when examined, are seen to be characteristic and such as would be difficult to invent. The reasonable hypothesis is to suppose that Beethoven did make certain claims for his music and that Elizabeth, very romantic and somewhat unscrupulous, gave them what she thought was an effective presentation.

The point is important because in this report is almost the only evidence we have as to Beethoven's conception of the function of music. It is a conception which was not consonant with the intellectual outlook of his own time, and which is, indeed, incompatible with the general intellectual climate of the last three centuries. We may assume, as the irreducible minimum basis of Elizabeth's fantasies, that Beethoven regarded art as a way of communicating knowledge about reality. Beethoven was a firm believer in what Mr. I. A. Richards[1] calls the "revelation theory" of art. This is a theory which, if true, means that art has a significance very much more important than that usually attributed to it. Art must rank with science and philosophy as a way of communicating knowledge about reality. Other artists besides Beethoven have held this view, but there is no room for it in the great scientific world outlook that was initiated in the seventeenth century and which is still the dominant outlook of our time. And a theory of æsthetics which is serious and does not simply ignore the great revolution in thought produced by science, finds it difficult, if not impossible, to attach to art the significance Beethoven claimed for it. Nevertheless, the fact that Beethoven, who created the music, held these

[1] *Principles of Literary Criticism.*

ideas about his music, is not unimportant. It seems easy for some writers, men of quite average sensibility and intelligence, to dismiss the testimony of the greatest artists to the meaning of their own work when this testimony conflicts with the philosophy the critic has found adequate to accommodate his own experience. Such an attitude shows a pathetic confidence in the validity of "established truths." A certain humility in the presence of utterances which presumably spring from a richer context of experience than we possess is surely to be excused. So that we may sympathize with Goethe when he replied to Elizabeth's report of Beethoven's conversation:—

> "The ordinary human mind might, perhaps, find contradictions in it; but before that which is uttered by one possessed of such a dæmon, an ordinary layman must stand in reverence, and it is immaterial whether he speaks from feeling or knowledge, for here the gods are at work strewing seeds for future discernment and we can only wish that they may proceed undisturbedly to development. But before they can become general, the clouds which veil the human mind must be dispersed. . . . To think of teaching him would be an insolence even in one with greater insight than mine, since he has the guiding light of his genius, which frequently illumines his mind like a stroke of lightning while we sit in darkness and scarcely suspect the direction from which daylight will break upon us."

The letter is a little constrained, but it is evident that Goethe feels that Beethoven must be treated with respect. It is impossible, Goethe feels, to be quite sure about the limitations of a genius of the Beethoven order. It would be advisable, then, before we dismiss Beethoven's ideas about the significance of music, to inquire into them more closely.

By the end of the eighteenth century the mental climate characteristic of the modern world was well established in the general mind. We have borrowed [1] the term "mental climate" to indicate those fundamental assumptions which are current during any particular period and which are the common ground, as it were, of the different world outlooks which are constructed during that period. Such assumptions do not exist as explicit philosophies; they are, rather, the basis of the philosophies created in their time. Such an assumption, unquestioned during the last three centuries, is, for example, that there exists an order of nature. The mental climate characteristic of the modern world is most clearly manifested in modern science, for here the activity is conditioned by the assumptions in a perfectly direct manner. But the same assumptions, for the most part unconscious, can be found in much modern philosophy and æsthetic criticism. For our present purpose the aspect of these assumptions that most interests us is that they make plausible the idea that art is an activity expressive wholly of peculiarities of the human constitution. It is

[1] A. N. Whitehead, *Science and the Modern World.*

7

not a revelation of reality; the values attributed by the artist to nature are not inherent in nature. The basis of this outlook is scientific materialism, which supposes that the reality of the world may be exhaustively described in terms of the abstractions found so successful in building up modern science—such abstractions as mass, force, location in space and time, and so on. In this universe the human mind, itself, in some way, the product of these abstractions, creates values expressive of its own constitution. These values are not part of reality; to suppose that they are is to adopt the "magical" view of the world. Our aspirations are expressive of nothing but our own needs—in the last resort, of our biological needs—and are, in that sense, purely accidental. They throw no light on the constitution of the universe; they point to no universal purpose in things. That the artist reveals to us the nature of reality, or anything but the peculiarities of his neural organization, is a notion incompatible with the scientific outlook on the world.

It follows from this that art is a somewhat trivial mystery. It is a mystery because the pleasure we indisputably get from a work of art cannot easily be related to our biological needs. Especially is this the case with music. It is difficult to understand why, in the struggle for existence, a peculiar sensibility to certain sequences of non-natural sounds should ever have been developed. And the mystery is trivial because nothing but an accidental and non-essential appetite appears to be involved. On the basis of this estimate of art the theory of "the æsthetic emotion" has been proposed. This theory supposes that amongst the emotions proper to a human

X sexual ?

8

being is one particular emotion which is excited by works of art or, more generally, by all "manifestations of the beautiful," and which is excited by nothing else. The emotion appears to be capable of degrees, but also of a maximum. Some works of art are better than others, but it is also possible for a work of art to be "perfect." The perfect work of art excites the æsthetic emotion to its maximum. The nearest analogy to this state would seem to be provided by the sexual orgasm. The classification of works of art proper on this theory, therefore, is the classification into perfect and imperfect, those that produce orgasm and those that do not. Amongst perfect works of art may be a symphony, a line of melody, an epic poem or a Serbian mat. The same value must naturally be attributed to all these works, since they are all completely successful in the function of a work of art, which is to excite the æsthetic emotion to its maximum. The objection to this theory is that it entirely fails to take into account the most important of our reactions to a work of art. It is not true that works of art excite in us one specific emotion, and works of art are not adequately classified as perfect and imperfect. The difference in our responses to a late quartet by Beethoven and an early quartet by Haydn, for instance, is not described by saying that a specific emotion is more or less excited. The one is not a more perfect form of the other. It may be replied that both compositions possess the quality of *beauty,* and that our only relevant reaction, from the point of view of æsthetic theory, is our reaction to this quality, a reaction which is susceptible of degrees, but which is always of the same kind. Such a reply derives all its plausibility merely from the poverty of language. Language, as an historical accident, is poor in names for subjective states, and consequently in names for the imputed properties of objects that produce those states. Even such words as love and hate, dealing with emotions to which mankind has always paid great attention, are merely portmanteau words. Within their meanings are not only differences of degree, but differences of kind. To conclude, because the word "beauty" exists almost in isolation, that it refers to some definite quality of objects, or that it is descriptive of some one subjective state, is to mistake a deficiency in language for a key to truth.

If we forgo the pleasing but puerile pastime of constructing a philosophy out of the accidents of grammar, and remain faithful to our actual experience, we shall find no reason to believe in a specific æsthetic emotion, nor to believe in the existence of some unique quality of beauty inhabiting all works of art. Such beliefs are merely the first and easiest steps in man's efforts to frame a theory of art which shall be compatible with the materialistic universe of science, in which values do not form part of reality. But it is quite possible for a truer and more flexible theory to flourish, even in this mechanistic desert. We need postulate no mystical similarity amongst works of art, nor suppose that one unique and apparently useless appetite is satisfied by them. We may admit the correctness of our direct perceptions that works of art are great and small, and not merely perfect and imperfect. The feeling we indisputably have, from a great work of art, that a large area of experience has been illuminated and harmonized for us, need not be wholly dismissed. It is true that experience is susceptible of different degrees of organization, and the superior degree of organization of his experience that has been achieved by a great artist may be, at least temporarily, communicated to us. We may suppose that his nervous system is, in some ways, better constructed than our own. He has not discovered and revealed some mystic quality of beauty; he has bestowed upon our experience a higher degree of organization. For the time being we see through his eyes. But, in order to remain faithful to materialism, we must not suppose that the artist has communicated knowledge; he has not given us a revelation about the nature of reality. Reality is the material of science, and values do not enter into the scientific scheme. The harmony of experience, as the artist reveals it, is not an indication that "all's right with the world"; it is merely an indication that his nervous system is organized in a certain way. The advantage of this theory over the "æsthetic emotion" theory is that it does not require us to do so much violence to the direct reactions we experience in the presence of a work of art. It is true that it does not allow us to take those reactions at their face value; we have, at least partially, to explain them away. But we are not required to reduce ourselves to the comparatively imbecile condition of the "pure æsthete." We are not required to pretend that a fine song is as valuable as a fine symphony, that comprehensiveness and profundity are as nothing compared with "perfection." The richness of the artist's material, and the extent and depth of his organization of it, are admitted to be the factors that give his work its value.

This theory is probably the most adequate that can be

devised on the basis of materialism. A work of art does not, as a scientific discovery does, exhibit new factors in reality; it merely presents a different and more desirable organization of experience from that we normally possess. This theory is, it must be admitted, a trifle obscure. If we think of the new ordering of known facts that a mathematical genius may give us we see that the distinction between organization of experience and the discovery of new factors in reality is not perfectly clear-cut. Probably a long and doubtful analysis would be required to make the point perfectly clear. This analysis, however, is not necessary, for there is reason to suppose that the materialistic doctrine on which the whole theory rests has no longer any compelling force.

The materialistic doctrine that has most influenced æsthetic theory is the doctrine that the artist's perceptions give us no knowledge of the nature of reality. This doctrine assumes that the whole of reality may be exhaustively described in terms of the fundamental scientific concepts elaborated in Europe during the seventeenth century. Stated thus nakedly the assumption seems an enormous one. The suspicion immediately arises that its ground is much more emotional than rational, but, in truth, the assumption did have a certain rational basis which has only recently been destroyed. That basis is found in the fact that the elements ignored by science never come in to disturb it. If other elements than those considered by science form an integral part of reality how is it that the scientific description seems to be complete? The fact that science forms a coherent and closed system is surely a presumption against the existence of what it ignores. By the end of the eighteenth century the convincing force of this argument was at its maximum. The triumphs achieved by the French mathematicians, on the basis of the concepts introduced by Galileo and made explicit by Newton, justified the belief that the key to the universe had now been discovered. Laplace's remark to Napoleon that in writing the *Mécanique Céleste,* he had found no need to assume the existence of God, expressed both the materialist position and the best available evidence for it. But this evidence was, after all, very slight. The fact that Laplace had not found God in the heavens was no proof that he would not find him on the earth. The phenomena of life and mind were so far from being included in the scientific scheme that it was only their almost total ignorance of these phenomena which enabled the eighteenth-century materialists to hope that they would be included. This objection can still be made to the materialist scheme; it has not yet shown itself competent to describe the whole of reality. But the objection has now acquired more force, for the great change that has come over the scientific outlook is due precisely to the fact that the materialist conceptions have been found to be inadequate in the very fields in which they achieved their greatest triumphs. And it is perfectly possible, in the resulting reorganization of scientific thought, that values will be regarded as inherent in reality. Even without this, however, recent analysis has resolved the paradox created by the fact that science forms a closed system. It has been shown that it does so in virtue of the fact that physics (the science on which the materialist outlook was based) deals with but one aspect of reality, namely, its structure, and remains perpetually within its own domain by the device of cyclic definition.

But for the purposes of a theory of art it is the fact that the materialist outlook has been abandoned rather than the reasons for its abandonment that is of importance. Our reactions to a work of art, or rather our interpretations of those reactions, have been largely conditioned by the mental climate brought about by scientific materialism. Nothing is more pervasive or more powerful than such a climate. It is indeed a climate in that it allows only certain growths to come to maturity, stunting and warping all others. The characteristic of this particular climate that interests us at present is that it has made difficult or impossible the correct evaluation of our æsthetic experiences and for this reason has hindered us in understanding the significance of a great artist. It has distorted our æsthetic perceptions by forcing us to accommodate them to a system of thought in which they really have no place, so that our reactions to a work of art are no longer accepted by us in their purity, but are immediately interpreted and sophisticated to serve our general outlook. For this reason most criticism is concerned with secondary issues, which are the only ones that can appear in the prevalent mental climate.

For the purposes of æsthetic criticism the most important fact that emerges from the present reorganization of scientific thought is that those elements of our experience that science ignores are not thereby shown to have no bearing upon the nature of reality. The fundamental concepts hitherto employed by science have been shown to be both unnecessary and insufficient. They are in process of being replaced by a different set, and it is perfectly possible that, when the replacement is complete, values will be established as inherent in reality. Even should science be able to progress without importing values into its scheme, that fact would afford no presumption against the existence of values. For one major result of recent physical speculation has been to show the precise nature of the limitations to scientific knowledge. Science gives us knowledge of structure, but not of substance. It may be assumed that this is the only kind of knowledge possible to us, but there seem to be no good reasons for such an assumption. Science, indeed, tells us a very great deal less about the universe than we have been accustomed to suppose, and there is no reason to believe that all we can ever know must be couched in terms of its thin and largely arbitrary abstractions.

With the disintegration of the three-centuries-old scientific outlook the way is clear for the construction of an adequate æsthetic criticism. It is ture, as Mr. Richards insists, that the artist gives us a superior organization of experience. But that experience includes perceptions which, although there is no place for them in the scientific scheme, need none the less be perceptions of factors in reality. Therefore a work of art may communicate knowledge. It may indeed be a "revelation." The "higher consciousness" of the great artist is evidenced not only by his capacity for ordering his experience, but also by having his experience. His world may differ from that of the ordinary man as the world of the ordinary man differs from that of a dog, in the extent of his contact with reality as well as in his superior organization of it. We may continue to maintain, then, the "revelation" theory of art. Indeed, our business as critics is to make it more explicit. The highest art has a transcendental function, as science has. In saying this, however, we must be careful to distinguish between these functions. We cannot say that art communicates knowledge, as science does, for we should be open to the objection made to the revelation theory of art that we cannot say what the revelation is of. But what art does do is to communicate to us an attitude, an attitude taken up by the artist consequent upon his perceptions, which perceptions may be perceptions of factors in reality. It is characteristic of the greatest art that the attitude it communicates to us is felt by us to be valid, to be the reaction to a more subtle and comprehensive contact with reality than we can normally make. We no longer need dismiss this feeling or attempt to explain it away. The colossal and mastered experience which seems to be reflected in the Heilgesang of the A minor quartet, for instance, is, we may be confident, indicative of more than the peculiarities of Beethoven's neural organization. The perceptions which made that experience possible were in no sense illusory; they were perceptions of the nature of reality, even though they have no place in the scientific scheme. Beethoven does not communicate to us his perceptions or his experiences. He communicates to us the attitude based on them. We may share with him that unearthy state where the struggle ends and pain dissolves away, although we know but little of his struggle and have not experienced his pain. He lived in a universe richer than ours, in some ways better than ours and in some ways more terrible. And yet we recognize his universe and find his attitudes towards it prophetic of our own. It is indeed our own universe, but as experienced by a consciousness which is aware of aspects of which we have but dim and transitory glimpses.

CHAPTER TWO

Music as Isolated

THE MOST formidable case that has yet been made out for the theory that music is meaningless has been presented by the late Edmund Gurney in his gigantic book *The Power of Sound.* This very able writer maintains that music is non-illustrative, that it is a form of Ideal Motion, and that it is apprehended by a special and isolated Musical Faculty. Except in the most flagrant examples of programme music the composer does not set out to express what Gurney calls "External objects and ideas." He does not even set out to express emotions. Music affords a delight which is *sui generis,* a delight which springs from the musical faculty's perception of ideal motion. The uniqueness and isolation of musical experiences is such that they cannot be either interpreted or described. Poets, painters and sculptors make reference to the external world; they may express ideas which can be interpreted, and situations that may be described. But the musician composes a sequence of sounds which have no reference to anything, and the actual sequence adopted is dictated wholly by his musical faculty. We class some sequences as good and some as bad, but this judgment is not based on any reference made by the music to external objects or ideas. The musical faculty approves of some sequences and condemns others, and that is all that can be said about the matter. It is true that music excites in us what may be called "musical emotions," but these have very little kinship with extra-musical emotions, that is, with emotions that may be aroused by something other than music.

Gurney seems to have been led to this position by the difficulty of saying what, if music means anything, it may be said to mean. He quotes the following analysis of Schubert's Unfinished symphony from the programme of a Philharmonic concert.

> "We begin with deep earnestness, out of which springs perturbation; after which almost painful anxieties are conjured up till the dissolution draws the veil from an unexpected solace, which is soon infused with cheerfulness, to be however abruptly checked. After an instant of apprehension, we are startled by a threat destructive to the very capability of rest, which in its turn subsides. From the terrible we pass to the joyful, and soon to playfulness and tenderness; a placid character which is quickly reversed by a tone of anger, continued till it leads up to a repetition of all that has gone before. Then comes the unfolding of a tale of passionate aspiration and depression, which works up to a culmination; after which some more repetition of the already twice-heard perturbation and what follows

it leads us to the final part, where, after being led in an unearthly way to abstract our thoughts from the present and its surroundings, we at last conclude in the strange mystery with which we set out, though just at the very end there is an effort to shut the mind against its incertitude."

As Gurney rightly remarks, Schubert could not possibly have set out to express the absurd jumble of emotions given in this "analysis." Schubert's Unfinished symphony impresses the hearer as being perfectly coherent, and even if we agree that the terms in this analysis, "playfulness," "depression" and so on, correspond to the musical emotions, their succession appears entirely arbitrary. We may say as much about almost any description of a musical composition. And it is a notorious fact that very different descriptions of the same composition will be given by different people. Gurney concludes, as we have said, that music does not depict extra-musical ideas and feelings at all. He assumes, in fact, that, since we cannot give names to our musical states, they must be unique. He further assumes that our musical states form, as it were, a closed system. A composer communicates to us his own musical states, and these testify to nothing but his musical perceptions. To reinforce his position he quotes the following remark from Mendelssohn.

"What any music *I* like expresses for me is not *thoughts too indefinite* to clothe in words, but *too definite*.—If you asked me what I thought on the occasion in question, I say, the song itself precisely as it stands. And if, in this or that instance, I had in my mind a definite word or definite words, I would not utter them to a soul, because words do not mean for one person what they mean for another; because the song alone can say to one, can awake in him, the same feelings it can in another—feelings, however, not to be expressed by the same words."

Gurney's doctrine, although less clearly and definitely, is professed by many musicians. Indeed, we may say that there are two main schools of musical philosophers, those who believe, like Wagner, that everything in heaven and earth is illuminated by music, and those who believe that music illuminates nothing whatever. Both positions impress one as unsatisfactory; it is impossible to be at ease as a whole-hearted adherent of either view. The idea that music testifies to nothing, in either the composer or the hearer, but the possession of a unique and isolated faculty, without reference to anything else in a man's nature, does violence to our most valued reactions to music. We do feel, in our most valued musical experiences, that we are making contact with a great spirit, and not simply with a prodigious musical faculty. On the other hand, no class of people is to be more avoided than those who look for, and find, a "story" in every musical composition.

One weakness of Gurney's theory is that it leaves unexplained the fact that there are a large number of people who do not accept it. If musical experiences are *sui generis,* having no reference to anything, how is it that reference has been attributed to them? Gurney tries to explain this on two grounds. He points out that a musical phrase often sounds like a statement, like *something said,* but he thinks this illusion quite explicable by the general association of music with speech. This explanation must certainly be rejected. The association of music and speech is of the slightest, and could not possibly be responsible for the marked effect noted by Gurney. Further, it would have to be shown that the melodic phrases which have this quality of affirmation are exceptionally akin, in pace and variation of pitch, to speech, and it is only necessary to select a few such phrases at random to see that this correspondence does not exist. Gurney's second ground is more general and tries to ac-account for the fact that some compositions, to many people, seem to have meaning. He suggests that such people are not really musical. There are many cultured people, quite able to appreciate the other arts, who are without the special musical faculty. Such people carry over, as it were, their educated habit of mind into their musical experiences. They are unable to experience music naïvely; their expectations, the result of their experience of the other arts, are all for meaning, for external references. They impute such references, therefore, to music, just as a child imputes various human attributes to a doll. Arguments of this kind always suffer from the disadvantage that they are susceptible of inversion. It would be quite impossible to prove that those people who find meaning in a composition are in all cases musically inferior to those who do not. At the same time it must be admitted that the meanings they discover are extremely various, and we can hardly suppose that the same musical composition has simultaneously several different meanings.

The problem is a genuine one and divides musicians, as it did in Gurney's time, into two camps. Its solution may be found by examining the statement that if music had meaning we must be able to say what that meaning is. We have already had occasion to point out that language is a limited, essentially practical instrument, particularly poor in names for subjective states. The number of subjective states that a man may experience is almost infinite. Not only music, but a landscape, poetry, an omnibus ride, can evoke countless experiences for which there are no names. The argument for the unique character of musical experiences will equally demonstrate the unique character of poetic experiences. The effect of a poem can no more be described than can the effect of a musical composition. To experience the effect the poem must be read and the composition must be heard. A description of a poem would seem just as inadequate as the description of Schubert's Unfinished symphony. Language, in poetry, expresses states for which language has no names except, perhaps, vague portmanteau names like triumph, joy, etc. It is true that the poem makes external references, but these references do not constitute the meaning of the poem. That meaning is to be found in the subjective state, or sequence of subjective states, that the poem expresses and communicates. Poetry, no more than music, can be paraphrased, but that fact does not testify to the existence of a unique and isolated poetic faculty. Poetic experiences are not isolated and without reference to anything else in the poet's spiritual make-up. On the contrary, they may be the synthetic, quintessential expressions of his whole nature and experience. In the same way, music may be expressive, and what it expresses is its meaning.

23

Musical phrases, like lines of poetry, are unique, but they are not thereby isolated. It is perfectly possible that there is a unique musical faculty, as unique as the sense of hearing itself, but it is not thereby an isolated faculty. Musical experiences do not form a closed world of their own. The highest function of music is to express the musician's experience and his organization of it. The whole man collaborates to make the composition. That the experience cannot be communicated in other terms is not surprising. Music shares this peculiarity with all the other arts. The reason that our reactions to a work of art cannot be adequately described is not that some unique and isolated faculty is involved, but that art is not superfluous, that it exists to convey what cannot be otherwise conveyed. Musical experiences, no more than poetic experiences, are isolated. It does not follow that they are not unique. It may be that our musical experiences, or some of them, cannot be evoked in any other way. But this is no more likely in the case of music than in the case of any of the other arts. Man's capacity of response, as it were, is almost infinite. It is perfectly possible that between certain reactions and stimuli there may be a one to one correspondence. A poem, in its effect upon us, may have no equivalent. A dawn or a sunset, a melody or a cry in the night, may evoke in us a reaction which is unique. It is even possible that most of our reactions, both to nature and to art, are unique. Art is no substitute for nature, and the arts are not substitutes for one another. Our commonest experiences, when they recur, recur with a difference. We do not fall in love twice in the same way. Even boredom has its shades. Mendelssohn's remark, quoted above, does no

24

more than assert the uniqueness of a musical experience.
Nevertheless, there are resemblances between unique
things, as in the case of two eggs. Mendelssohn thinks
words too vague and indefinite to convey his musical
experience of the song, but he would agree that some
combinations of words come nearer than some others to
expressing his experience. Amongst our musical experiences are some which are more analogous than others to
certain extra-musical experiences. These experiences
need not be more or less valuable than those musical experiences for which we can find no analogues. The
strictly unique character of musical experiences is a
rather trivial fact about them. But that they exist in
isolation would be, if true, a very important characteristic. For it would follow that music exists to do nothing
but employ, agreeably, a special faculty. The musician's
experience of life and what he has made of it, the extent
and depth of his inner life, could find, on this theory, no
reflection in his music. A more meaningless and irrelevant addendum to life than music could not well be
conceived. The pleasures of the wine-bibber could be
ranked as high, for what they may lose in intensity they
probably make up in usefulness, by promoting truthfulness and aiding digestion. Music thus becomes the most
trivial of the arts, and the musician the least self-revela-
tory of all artists. As this conclusion is quite incompatible with our judgments of the value of our musical
experiences we must investigate their nature more
closely.

CHAPTER THREE

Music as Expression

WE HAVE seen that there is no reason to believe that uniqueness implies isolation. Poetic experiences are quite as unique as musical experiences, but nobody imagines that they form a closed world of their own, that they are wholly dissociated from the rest of the poet's nature and from his experience of life. It is true that, for the appreciation of a work of art in any medium, special sensibilities are required, and such sensibilities can be pleasurably exercised in almost complete independence of any other interests. Thus much of Spenser's poetry may perhaps be regarded as existing in a moral and spiritual vacuum; it has, so to say, almost no discoverable context. Here the specific poetic sensibilities are being exercised "for their own sakes." Music, much more than poetry, affords specimens of works which lead this curiously independent existence, but it need be no more true of music than of poetry that it must be essentially meaningless. If, therefore, we find that some compositions irresistibly suggest to us some spiritual context we need not resist this impulse on theoretical grounds. We need not suppose that we are the victims of a literary culture and an imperfectly developed musical faculty. As a matter of fact, all the greatest music in the world, and some of the worst, does suggest a spiritual context. It does more than suggest; its whole being is conditioned by this context, and it lives to express it. This context is directly perceived even by those who, for theoretical reasons, do not explicitly admit its existence. The most ardent advocate of the isolation theory will, for example, describe one composition as more "profound" than another, will describe one melody as "noble" and another as "sentimental." Such judgments are incompatible with the isolation theory, for on that theory nothing could be said except that a piece of music afforded a greater or less degree of a unique and incommunicable pleasure. A composition could be no more profound or noble or sentimental than a wine. Yet such judgments, in the case of many compositions, are quite unavoidable.

If this be admitted we may, for our present purposes, divide musical compositions into three classes. We may admit that, so far as our present analysis penetrates, there are compositions which exist in isolation. Secondly, there are compositions which spring from a spiritual context and express spiritual experiences. And, thirdly, there is the class of music ordinarily called programme music. Of these classes the second is the most important.

In our reactions to compositions belonging to the first group we find that nothing is involved but our perceptions of musical quality and the delight those perceptions afford. An analysis of these perceptions could only be undertaken on the basis of a theory of musical æsthetics, and no satisfactory theory exists. No theory that has yet been proposed, such as Darwin's theory that music is a highly developed form of the sexual calls of animals, or Spencer's theory that it is an elaboration of emotional speech, gives any explanation of why one musical phrase is pleasing and another not nor, more important still, why one sequence of phrases seems satisfactory, stimulating and "logical," while another sequence appears arbitrary and boring. It is possible that, in the remote future, the physiology of the nervous system will throw some light on the matter, but at present it is impossible to give any recipes for writing good melodies or for developing a musical theme in a satisfactory manner. The rules which have from time to time been propounded, based on the examination of large numbers of examples, are as faithfully obeyed by bad music as by good. What is quite certain is that musical phrases differ in quality and that successions of phrases differ in the degree of their musical fitness and coherence. Whether any music really exists which involves *only* these perceptions we are not here concerned to argue. We are prepared to admit that, so far as our analysis extends, there are compositions which appeal only to our musical perceptions of quality and coherence, variety, invention, and so on, leaving it to the science of the future to say what connection these musical perceptions may have with the rest of our perceptions.

Our response to music of the second kind involves more factors than does our response to music of the first kind. Music which impresses us as expressing spiritual

X "Art of Fugue"

28

experiences and as springing from a spiritual context is still music. It must satisfy the musical faculty; it must obey all the criteria that "pure" music obeys. But the musical experiences it communicates are less isolated than those of pure music; a greater extent, as it were, of the artist's nature has been concerned in their creation; more comprehensive and, probably, deeper needs are satisfied by them. Amongst musical phrases are some which do more than please our musical faculty. They stir other elements in us; they reverberate throughout a larger part of our being. Certain emotions and expectations are aroused beside those that accompany our reactions to pure music. And the sequences of such phrases, besides satisfying our musical faculty's criteria of coherence and fitness, also satisfy these other expectations, give a natural development to these other emotions, continue, by a process of organic growth, this wilder life that has been awakened in us. But the poverty of language in names for subjective states has tempted many writers to describe these experiences, communicated to us by music, by describing some situation or event which would, they think, arouse a similar response. And because such situations are very largely conditioned by the critic's sensibility and imagination the same composition may be given a great apparent variety of interpretations. But, in any case, the bare statement of a situation the composition is supposed to be about tells us nothing of any value. Even if the composer had a definite situation in mind, and one knew precisely what that situation was, a description of the situation tells us nothing of the quality of the response awakened by the music.

29

x "art"

x or true subjectivity outside of one's objective self

Beethoven's imaginative realization of the death of a hero, in the slow movement of the Eroica symphony, for instance, is utterly different in quality from Wagner's realization of the same situation in the Siegfried funeral march. What these compositions mean to us is precisely their communication, in each case, of the personal and individual conception of the situation. And it is this personal conception which reveals to us directly the depth and subtlety of the composer's feelings and perceptions. Such communications inform us directly of the spiritual context from which they spring, and they do this even if we are completely ignorant of any situation that may be involved. On the other hand, knowledge of the situation tells us nothing that we want to know. If we use the word "heroic" to describe the music of the Eroica symphony, that is not because the symphony is "about" Napoleon or Abercrombie, but because Heroism, as a state of being, was realized by Beethoven to the extent that he has expressed it, and it is the quality of his realization that is important. It is *his* conception of the heroic that matters to us, and which is a clue to the greatness of the soul which is expressing itself. The comparative tawdriness of Wagner's music is not due to any difference there might be in the imagined situation, but to the comparative poverty of his inner resources.

A knowledge of the situation that a musical composition is "about," therefore, can tell us little of value. And in practice we almost always know nothing of the situation, if any, that was in the mind of the composer. Nevertheless, a great deal of writing on music consists in presentations of imagined situations, and this is one reason why writing on music is properly classed as one of the dreariest branches of literature. It is possible that a great literary artist could so select and present a situation that experiences similar to those evoked by a given composition would be experienced by the reader. Beethoven, for instance, when asked for the "meaning" of the Appassionata sonata told his questioner to read Shakespeare's *Tempest*. No two compositions could be more unlike, and Beethoven was either joking or knew nothing of the play but its title. But he could, with more point, have referred a questioner to *Macbeth* as an illustration of the first movement of the C minor symphony. Even such vague correspondences are rare, however, and the usual "programme" presented by the writer on music seems to have little more relation to the composition than would a newspaper report of a street accident. But just as the journalist may have had emotions justifying his use of the word "Tragedy," so these programmes may represent something to their authors. These strange landscapes and violent variations in the weather conditions that so many compositions seem to suggest are, we may suppose, the symbols for experiences that are less trivial than they seem. They are merely unsuccessful devices of communication. We cannot know, for instance, what significance dancing elves, murmuring brooks and thunderstorms may have in the imagination of the descriptive writer. Such programmes are merely unintelligible. A man thinks of what symbols he can, and the symbols he invents are conditioned not only by his sensibility and imagination, but by his experience. To this is due the great variety of interpretations of the same composition. It is possible that the different interpreters had similar spiritual experiences evoked by the composition, but it requires a great artist to express such experiences unambiguously. We may conclude then, that it is very doubtful whether any compositions of the kind we are discussing are "about" any of the programmes that have been suggested for them. And as we have said, if we did know the programme we should know nothing of importance about the composition. The "meaning" of these compositions is to be found in the spiritual experiences they evoke. The musical critic who wishes to describe these experiences is faced with precisely the same task as the literary critic who wishes to describe the significance of a poem and, like the literary critic, he is likely to achieve but a stammering success. But his task is no harder. Both critics should eschew "programmes" as irrelevant, although as the situation is explicit in a poem it is much easier to regard it as vital. But it is really no more illuminating to be told that Wordsworth wrote a sonnet about the view of London from Westminster Bridge than it is to be told that Chopin wrote a waltz about a puppy chasing its tail. The difference is that the poet himself cannot express his reaction to the situation without mentioning the situation, whereas the musician can do so. Music, compared with the other arts, is a kind of disembodied ghost, and has all the advantages and disadvantages of that state.

The reluctance of many musicians to admit that music of the kind we are discussing (which includes almost the whole of Beethoven's music) is in any sense programme music is due to their feeling that any proposed "situation" is not only inadequate but even irrelevant. In denying the adequacy of any proposed situation to the musical effect they have been led to the strained position that music has no extra-musical content whatever, that it witnesses to nothing in the composer except his possession of an isolated faculty called musical imagination. This view, as we have said, is not compatible with our direct reactions to music, and even the exponents of this view seem to find it almost impossible, as their writings prove, to hold it consistently. It is also in direct contradiction to the expressed views of some of the great composers themselves. Beethoven most certainly regarded his music as expressing states of consciousness which might conceivably have been expressed by some other art. Indeed, he seems to have regarded music not only as a medium for the presentation of "beauty," but as a language with which he was more familiar than any other. The evidence of his letters and reported remarks is quite clear on this point. Thus, in describing his method of composition to Louis Schlosser he refers to himself as "incited by moods, which are translated by the poet into words, by me into tones that sound, and roar and storm about me until I have set them down in notes." And in conversation with Neate he said: "I always have a picture in my mind when composing, and follow its lines." That we are not to take the word "picture" in this remark too literally is shown by his letter of July 15, 1817, to Wilhelm Gerhard where he says: "The description of a picture belongs to the field of painting; in this the poet can count himself more fortunate than my muse for his territory is not so restricted as mine in this respect, though mine, on the other hand, extends into other regions, and my dominion is not easily reached." And Schindler reports that Beethoven, in his later years, complained that people were less able to grasp the meaning of music than they were in his young days, and he even thought of giving poetic titles to his earlier works to supply this deficiency in his hearers' imaginations. It is certain, therefore, that Beethoven, at any rate, considered that his music had an extra-musical content, that is to say, a content that could conceivably be expressed in some other medium. But we may be quite certain that whatever poetic titles Beethoven or anybody else had given to his compositions would not have assisted his hearers in grasping this content. For the content, as we have said, is the composer's reaction to the situation, not the situation. And this reaction is conditioned by the spiritual nature of the man and is a revelation of it. In his capacity to express this content Beethoven reveals himself as a great musical genius, and the content itself reveals him as a great spirit.

Music, as an expressive art, evokes states of consciousness in the hearer which are analogous to states that may be produced by extra-musical means. It is usual to describe these states as "emotions" but this word, unless carefully used, is misleading. Psychologists have tabulated human emotions, that is, they have given a list of those emotions for which names exist. But it is difficult to find a musical composition whose effect is adequately described as evoking one or more of these emotions. No composition, for instance, can be adequately described as "melancholy" or "joyful." Such emotions, if they enter at all into the total effect, never enter as isolated elements. Gurney has proposed the term "fused emotion" to describe the musical experience, but the term is not very illuminating. We are again in presence of the mystery that attends our reaction to any work of art. There are as few melancholy or joyful poems as there are musical compositions. It may be that our reaction to a work of art is a synthesis of relatively simple emotions, but the analysis would probably teach us little. For the effect exists as a whole and not as an assemblage of its elements, just as a living creature is more than an assemblage of its constituent molecules. Such synthetic wholes are doubtless the highest experiences of which we are capable, but they are probably too rare and of too little practical importance to have received names. There is no harm in calling them emotions, provided it is realized that we are only rarely referring to named emotions. Some fairly complex emotions, such as "awe," have received names and have been more or less plausibly analysed into a number of simpler constituent emotions. But our reactions to a work of art have hitherto resisted analysis into these simple terms, and for that reason many people have supposed that some unique "æsthetic emotion" is involved. But we have already objected to that theory that it does not account for the differences in our reactions to different works of art.

The most valuable states or "emotions" that music arouses are those that spring from the richest and deepest spiritual context. We are immediately aware, with great compositions of this kind, that the state of consciousness expressed by the composer is the result of certain perceptions and experiences. So far as we can recognize the emotion communicated to us we can say something of the conditions it, as it were, presupposes. If there is nothing in our experience akin to that of the composer his composition can be for us nothing but an example of "pure music." But the experiences we attribute to the composer tell us nothing, of course, about the causes of those experiences. To suppose that they do is to fall into the error of the programme writer. Thus when Marx describes the A minor quartet as inspired by Beethoven's progress from a sick bed to health we feel that the description is both inadequate and arbitrary. He has failed to do justice to the quality of the experience from which the work sprang, and he has quite arbitrarily invented a cause of the experience. But the critic who should deny any spiritual content whatever to the A minor quartet, who should fail to see that it could only germinate in the soil of some profound experience, would fail even more signally than Marx.

The function of the kind of music we have been discussing is to communicate valuable spiritual states, and these states testify to the depth of the artist's nature and to the quality of his experience of life. Such states cannot usually be correlated with definite situations, and for that reason no programme for them can be given. They are the fruits of countless experiences as realized and coordinated by the artist, and they enter into the very texture of his spiritual being. But there are certain classes of experiences, not perhaps of the highest order, for which situations can be assigned. Music expressing such experiences, deliberately relating them to the situation, is the highest form of what is ordinarily called programme music. We may take Beethoven's Pastoral symphony as being, on the whole, a composition of this class. It is concerned, for the most part, to depict its composer's reactions to various pastoral scenes. But, together with this, it contains a good deal of programme music of a different order whose purpose it is to give a musical representation of certain physical perceptions. The notorious cuckoo notes, the effect of flowing water in the Beside the Brook movement, the storm, are specimens of music of this class. It would not be sufficient to say of such music that its purpose is to represent physical perceptions. The representation must be musical, and only as realistic as is compatible with that condition. This means that the representation can never be completely realistic except when the physical perceptions concerned are musical sounds. Thus a tolling bell can be represented very realistically by tolling a bell. But it is only the most stupid modern composers who give equally realistic representations of trains and motor-horns. In any case, the actual physical perceptions that can be communicated by music are very few, although there is evidence that music can, for some people, suggest other than auditory perceptions. Thus there can be no doubt that, for some minds, sounds and colours are associated. Many lists have been given of the colour equivalents of the different orchestral instruments. The lists do not agree, but that does nothing to invalidate the existence of the correspondences. Even keys have their characteristic colours for some minds. It is possible, therefore, that by correct choice of key and instrumentation compositions could be designed which would powerfully suggest to such minds certain landscape effects. We also find that some music irresistibly reminds certain musical critics of food. Or it may arouse olfactory images. Writings on music abound in which colours, wines, peaches and perfumes are suggested to the authors by musical compositions. But such powers of evocation belong to the more freakish resources of music. No compositions worth talking about are designed to arouse such images, and probably those who experience them would regard them as amongst the least valuable of their reactions to the music. Such by-products of auditory stimuli do not help us to understand the peculiar character of programme music. That character does not consist in any correspondences that may exist between auditory and other physical perceptions, but in the analogy between the musical emotions communicated and the emotions aroused by the external situation that forms the programme of the composition. If it be said, for instance, that Debussy's L'Après-midi d'un Faune makes the impression of "a vegetable world alive in quivering hot sunshine . . . the life of trees, streams and lakes, the play of light upon water and on clouds, the murmur of plants drinking and feeding in the sunlight," it is not because musical sounds can evoke images of heat and light and vegetables, but because a man in such surroundings may typically experience emotions analogous to those communicated by the music. Programme music, in the strict sense, may be defined as music that communicates musical experiences analogous to extra-musical experiences that may be associated with some definite external situation. It does not, any more than any other music, depict any part of the external world.

BOOK TWO

Beethoven's Spiritual Development

CHAPTER ONE

Beethoven's Characteristics

ONE of the most significant facts, for the understanding of Beethoven, is that his work shows an organic development up till the very end. The older Beethoven lived, the more and more profound was what he had to say. The greatest music Beethoven ever wrote is to be found in the last string quartets, and the music of every decade before the final period has greater music than its predecessor. Such sustained development, in the case of an artist who reaches years of maturity, is a rare and important phenomenon. Bach, for instance, who may be likened to Beethoven for the seriousness and maturity of his mind, lost himself at the end in the arid labyrinths of pure technique. Wagner, as the fever in his blood grew less, had nothing to express at the end but exhaustion and ineffectual longing. Beethoven's music continually developed because it was the expression of an attitude towards life that had within it the possibility of indefinite growth.

41

Some attitudes towards life are not susceptible of development. They may achieve greater richness and subtlety, but they are incapable of organic growth. The cynic, for example, may become more bitter and penetrating, but unless he suffers a catastrophic change he remains at the same distance from reality. The man who has sincerely accepted a religious scheme in which all the major problems of life are provided with solutions is likely to go through life without ever experiencing the direct impact of those problems. That is, in fact, the weakness of Bach as compared with Beethoven. Wagner, the great apostle of the pride of life, finds, as the bright world slips past him, that he is left alone with his yearning and his pain. The attitude of both Bach and Wagner towards life was not sufficient to support all their length of days. Beethoven, on his death-bed, could say, *Plaudite, amici, comœdia finita est.* But the "comedy" has been in play up to the last moment.

The chief characteristics of the fully mature Beethoven's attitude towards life are to be found in his realization of suffering and in his realization of the heroism of achievement. The character of life as suffering is an aspect that our modern civilization, mercifully for the great majority of people, does a great deal to obscure. Few men have the capacity fully to realize suffering as one of the great structural lines of human life. Bach, as we have said, escaped the problem with his religious scheme. Wagner, on the basis of a sentimental philosophy, finds the reason and anodyne of suffering in the pity it awakens. Mozart, with his truer instinct, is bewildered. The G minor quintet is the most poignant expression of his angelic anguish at his late discovery of this earth's pain. To Beethoven the character of life as suffering became a fundamental part of his outlook. The deep sincerity and *naïveté* of his nature, combined with the circumstances of his life, made this knowledge inevitable. The quality of this realization has nothing in common with the pessimism of such a man as Schopenhauer. It is the direct, simple and final acceptance of an obvious fact. This attitude of mind is perhaps rarer to-day than at any previous period in history. To the modern mind suffering is essentially remediable. Suffering is primarily due to physical and moral maladjustment, and with the spread of science and correct social theories we shall be able to abolish it. For an increasing number of people suffering is already practically abolished. They may go through life without meeting one problem they cannot evade until they reach their death-bed, while they find the sufferings of others easier to endure through their conviction that they are the temporary consequences of the imperfect state of society. But to the vast majority of people suffering is still one of the fundamental characteristics of life, and it is their realization that an experience of suffering, pure and profound, enters as an integral part into Beethoven's greatest work, that helps to give that work its unique place in the minds and hearts of men.

Beethoven's capacity for a deep and passionate realization of suffering necessitated, if he were not to be reduced to impotence, a corresponding capacity for endurance and an enormous power of self-assertion. No artist ever lived whose work gives a greater impression of indomitable strength than we find in some of Beethoven's most characteristic movements. The force that triumphs throughout the Scherzo of the ninth symphony, for example, is indeed indestructible, while the fugue of the Hammerclavier sonata is an almost insensate outburst of unconquerable self-assertion. As he grew older his force increased. "I will take Fate by the throat," he said as a young man, à propos of his increasing deafness, and there is plenty of the "will to victory" in the fifth symphony he proceeded to write. But a stronger, although a more subtle pulse, is to be found in some of the last string quartets. In his last years he had more to carry and he carried it more lightly.]

The "personality" of such a man as Beethoven is a slowly developed synthetic whole. It is formed by the gradual combination of its constituent elements into an organic unity. For the development of a personality a rich and profound inner life is necessary, and for that reason it is usually only great artists and religious teachers who impress us as being complete persons. Amongst the elements constitutive of Beethoven's personality we must include his lack of malleability. This quality made him almost immune from purely external influences. Thus he was impervious to criticism; his manners were atrocious; he ignored conventions; he was permanently subject to no social passions, not even sexual love. The low standard of education he achieved seems to have been as much due to his lack of plasticity as to his lack of opportunities. He was not an educable man. He accepted none of the schemes of thought or conduct current in his time; it is doubtful whether he was even fully aware of their existence. He remained utterly faithful to his own experience. It is for this reason that his affirmative utterances, as in the Credo of the

Mass in D, have such unexampled weight. Such utterances spring solely from his own personal and tested experience.

Beethoven's capacity for realizing the fundamental character of life in its two aspects of suffering and achievement, combined with his lack of flexibility, was the necessary condition for the development of his attitude towards life. That development takes the form of a synthesis. The Beethoven of the C minor symphony finds the meaning of life in achievement in spite of suffering. Fate is an enemy to be defied. The Beethoven of the last quartets finds that the highest achievement is reached through suffering. Suffering is accepted as a necessary condition of life, as an illuminating power. That the reconciliation he thus effected was genuine and complete is made evident by the music, for none of Beethoven's music is more obviously the expression of an authentic experience. The quality of this experience has led many writers to call this music "mystical" or "metaphysical." But whatever meanings these terms may be intended to convey, the music in question is really Beethoven's expression of the final synthesis he achieved between the primary elements of his experience. He did not turn away from life towards some mystical Nirvana. He forgot none of the joy, the effort, or the pain. He abandoned nothing. What he achieved is something much more wonderful than an old man's serenity. The life in the last string quartets is as full, varied and intense as anywhere in Beethoven's music. But those aspects of life that Beethoven formerly presented as contrasted he now presents as harmoniously flowering from a single stem. Life's experiences are still presented with all their diversity, but no longer as conflicting.

Within the iron framework of Beethoven's permanent attitude towards life flourished a highly sensitive and passionate emotional nature. Although his vision had the stern strength of the Puritan outlook it had none of its bleakness. He was fully alive to the countless lovely and tender things in life. No one's reaction to simple pastoral scenes, for example, was ever more intense and innocent than Beethoven's. He had none of the doubts that troubled the Victorian romantics after their acquaintance with the doctrine of the "struggle for existence," neither had he any of the eighteenth-century cultured affectation of a "love for nature." His reaction was spontaneous, direct and unsophisticated. Only a man pure in heart could have written the Pastoral symphony. The same quality is shown in what may be called his love music. The Op. 78 sonata expresses that exquisite, shy and yet joyful tenderness, that only the truly chaste have ever achieved. In this it is typical. In spite of music's unexampled power of expressing eroticism, most powerfully exemplified by Wagner's work, there is no trace of this quality in Beethoven. He knows nothing, even in his most abandoned mood (as in the finale of the seventh symphony) of the ecstasy of sexual delirium. We know from Beethoven's own words that he was what is called a "moralist" in sexual matters, but we know from his music that this was due to no asceticism, to no principles, but to the presence of very strong feelings which could allow nothing inferior in that kind to co-exist with them. To the man of the world Beethoven's love for music may be that of a romantic; to the youth who is just awakening to the awe and rapture of this great experience Beethoven is one of the very few true poets of the heart. Beethoven's attitude towards sexual love never became sophisticated. This very intense and rich emotional nature was, in truth, very simple and very pure. There were no feigned or borrowed emotions, and nerve-storms never took the place of feelings. He had no need to complicate his joy with bitterness or to distort his rapture with cynicism. These are the devices of a man who wishes to come to terms with his suffering without facing it in all its starkness. But Beethoven had the innocence of his courage.

We have, then, in the person of Beethoven a musical genius with all the conditions for writing great music. He has a realization of the ultimate character of life, he has a force adequate to any trial, however arduous, his growth will be free from the distorting effects of mere convention, and his response is pure and sincere to a wide range of experience. No other musician who ever lived has united so many advantages.

The mystery of the appearance of what Goethe called *"eine Natur"* in contrast to a *"süsse Puppe,"* is not to be resolved by any discussion of heredity and environment. For the chief characteristic of a person—a "personality" —is that it is a synthetic, an organic, whole, and not a mere collection of its constituent elements. If we could trace every one of Beethoven's characteristics in his ancestry, we still should be in no position to "reconstruct" Beethoven. But, in fact, there is very little that is characteristic of Beethoven to be found in his ancestry. It must be remembered, of course, that we know very little about his ancestry. It has been traced back to the beginning of the seventeenth century and to a small village in Belgium near Louvain. But, for the most part, these people have left no record of themselves beyond their names and the dates of those events in their lives that are of interest to the State. We know that the family produced a painter, a sculptor, and a curé, and that the commercial enterprise with which it was most prominently associated was the wine trade. The first ancestor about whom we have a fair amount of information is the grandfather, Ludwig van Beethoven, born in 1712. This Ludwig came to Bonn, at the age of nineteen, as singer in the court chapel, and steadily rose in his profession until, in 1761, he became "Herr Kapellmeister." He must have been a man with a character that inspired respect, for he was appointed to this position in spite of the fact that he was not a composer. Beethoven always spoke of this ancestor with particular respect and, indeed, in his vigour and integrity he was not unlike Beethoven. It is probable that the old man had a good deal of the same "moralistic" outlook although, as he was not a creative artist, we cannot tell on what perceptions and realizations it was based. In any case, he is the only ancestor we can point to as showing any resemblance to Beethoven at all. It is possible, nevertheless, that Beethoven derived more elements from his grandmother and father. We have no direct evidence for this, but it is significant that both were habitual drunkards. Habitual drunkenness is usually, psychologists inform us, the result of an inability to accommodate oneself wholly to reality. It is often a vice in that unfortunate class of people who have imperfectly co-ordinated artistic faculties. They yearn vaguely for something other than the world they know, but they lack the capacity to create a world nearer to their heart's desire. Still more do they lack the capacity to attain a comprehensive vision of the beauty immanent in this world. Neither the art of escape nor the art of revelation is possible to them. Nevertheless, they have perceptions they cannot use and impulses that never come to fruition. Drink, or some other drug, by relieving their sense of impotence and by blurring the unfriendly outlines of the real world, brings them solace and becomes a necessity. In the case of the father we know that he had fair musical abilities, quite equal to the grandfather's, although nothing sufficient to justify any great ambition. And he appears to have been of the weak, gradually deteriorating type, not in the least the headstrong passionate drunkard. He was a shiftless, feebly unscrupulous man. He presents many of the characteristics of the impotent dreamer type and certainly, if we are to account for Beethoven by any theory of heredity, something is needed to leaven the solid common sense and practical grasp of life shown by the grandfather. Of Beethoven's mother we know even less. She may actually have been a rather colourless person, or this impression may be due to the conventional, indiscriminating language of the accounts we have of her. We learn that she was "always serious," a "quiet, suffering woman," pious, gentle and amiable, and that she was much liked and respected. It is certain that the boy Beethoven loved her passionately; it is also pretty clear that he confided to her nothing of what was fermenting in his young mind. It was her patience, gentleness and suffering that moved the boy to such an agony of tenderness. "What is marriage?" she said once; "at first a little

49

X excellent

joy, then a chain of sorrows." If we imagine Madame Beethoven as the passively enduring, suffering woman she seems to have been, we can understand the special feeling with which Beethoven always referred to her. The profoundest love of such a man is always based on compassion. More virile types, where no sex interest was concerned, would get little from Beethoven but his best wishes.

The traceable resemblance between Beethoven and his ancestry is, then, of the slightest. But the actual circumstances of his early life do much more to make clear to us certain characteristics of the mature man. The fundamental characteristics we have already described are not, of course, to be illuminated in this way. There is no reason to suppose that Beethoven would have written like Mendelssohn if the circumstances of his life had been as happy as Mendelssohn's. A capacity for realizing the character of life is not created, but only exercised, by particular occasions. Mendelssohn, in some circumstances, might have been reduced to impotence; he would never have become a tragic poet. From the point of view of Beethoven's development he had what can only be regarded as favourable surroundings in his early years. They were undesirable, as his deafness was calamitous, only from the point of view of his personal happiness. From the point of view of mankind at large they were advantages. It must certainly be counted an advantage, for instance, that Beethoven should so early have been pushed on to acquire a considerable degree of self-reliance. When, in the early twenties, he went to Vienna, it was with a courageous self-confidence commensurate with his power and originality, a self-confidence very necessary for the full safeguarding of that originality. This unusual degree of maturity is the more explicable if we remember that Beethoven occupied a fairly important musical position even at the age of twelve years. Besides being assistant organist to Neefe he was also "cembalist in the theatre," a position of considerable honour and responsibility. He owed his position largely to the fact that his father, inspired by the dazzling career of the young Mozart, endeavoured to exploit Beethoven as an infant prodigy. The father's methods of achieving this end were certainly harsh. Sometimes the boy would be dragged from bed late at night, on his father's return from the local inn, and forced to practise the clavier. The father required unremitting industry, which he secured by the threat and practice of punishment. Outside music, however, the father cared nothing for the boy's education. The only school Beethoven attended, and then only for a short time, was a lower grade public school in Bonn called the Tirocinium. His fellow-student, Wurzer, remembered him as dirty and uncared for. But Beethoven refused to blossom into an infant prodigy of the Mozart order. The father did the best he could by falsifying the boy's age, giving it out that he was born in 1772 instead of 1770, but, even so, the performances of the young Beethoven, remarkable as they must have been, by no means reached the standard set by the young Mozart. Yet that the boy was fairly precocious is shown by Neefe's communication, dated March 2, 1783, to *Cramer's Magazine*. He speaks of

> "Louis von Beethoven, son of the tenor singer mentioned, a boy of eleven years and of most promising talent. He plays the clavier very skilfully and

with power, reads at sight very well, and—to put it in a nutshell—he plays chiefly 'The Well-Tempered Clavichord' of Sebastian Bach, which Herr Neefe put into his hands. Whoever knows this collection of preludes and fugues in all the keys—which might almost be called the *non plus ultra* of art—will know what this means. So far as his duties permitted, Herr Neefe has also given him instruction in thorough-bass. He is now training him in composition and for his encouragement has had nine variations for the pianoforte, written by him on a march—by Ernst Christolph Dressler—engraved at Mannheim. This youthful genius is deserving of help to enable him to travel. He would surely become a second Wolfgang Amadeus Mozart were he to continue as he has begun."

It is probable, therefore, that the father never entirely abandoned hope of profiting by his son's ability, and Thayer's conjecture that the father inspired Beethoven's futile expedition to Vienna, in the spring of 1787, to take lessons from Mozart, is not unreasonable.

Of Beethoven's life from the year 1784 to the spring of 1787 we know practically nothing. The motive of his visit to Vienna at this latter date can only be guessed at. It is possible that the boy, then sixteen years of age, had become sufficiently conscious of his power to feel irked by the narrow opportunities offered him at Bonn. All that is known certainly is that his visit to Vienna was a short one, that he took a few lessons from Mozart, and that he had to borrow money on his journey back. His letter to Schaden of Augsburg, from whom he had borrowed the money, explains the circumstances, and also affords evidence of the exceptional maturity that had been achieved by this boy of sixteen.

"I can easily imagine what you must think of me, and I cannot deny that you have good reasons for an unfavourable opinion. I shall not, however, attempt to justify myself, until I have explained to you the reason why I hope my apologies will be accepted. I must tell you that from the time I left Augsburg my cheerfulness as well as my health began to decline; the nearer I came to my native city the more frequent were the letters from my father urging me to travel with all possible speed as my mother was not in a favourable state of health. I therefore hurried forward as fast as I could, although myself far from well. My longing once more to see my dying mother overcame every obstacle and assisted me in surmounting the greatest difficulties. I found my mother still alive but in the most deplorable state; the disease was consumption, and about seven weeks ago, after much pain and suffering, she died. She was such a kind, loving mother to me, and my best friend. Ah, who was happier than I when I could still utter the sweet name, mother, and it was heard? And to whom now can I speak it? Only to the silent image resembling her evoked by the power of the imagination. I have passed very few pleasant hours since my arrival here, having during the whole time been suffering from asthma, which may, I fear, eventually develop into consumption; to this is added melancholy—almost as great an evil as my malady itself. Imagine yourself in my place, and then I shall hope to receive your forgiveness for my long silence. You showed me extreme kindness and friendship by lending me three Carolins in Augsburg, but I must entreat your indulgence for a time. My journey cost me a great deal, and I have not the smallest hopes of earning anything here. Fate is not propitious to me in Bonn.

"Pardon my detaining you so long with my chatter; it was necessary for my justification.

"I do entreat you not to deprive me of your valuable friendship; nothing do I wish so much as in some degree to become worthy of your regard.

"I am, with the highest respect,

"Your most obedient servant and friend,

"L. v. BEETHOVEN,

"Court Organist to the Elector
of Cologne."

The family was at this time in the direst poverty. Shortly before the death of his wife the father had petitioned the Elector for aid, mentioning that he had been compelled to sell a portion of his effects and to pawn others, and that he no longer knew what to do for his sick wife and many children, but there is no evidence that his petition was granted. The "many" children numbered four, Beethoven and his two brothers Carl and Johann, and an infant sister, Margareth, who died in the November of this same year. There was thus good reason for the "melancholy" mentioned by Beethoven. Even the most pressing needs could be met only through the good offices of a family friend, the violinist Franz Ries. Some thirteen years after, when Ferdinand Ries, the son of Franz, presented a letter of introduction from his father to Beethoven in Vienna, Beethoven read the letter and said: "I cannot answer your father just now;

but do you write to him that I have not forgotten how my mother died. He will be satisfied with that."

Beethoven, his father and two brothers, continued to live together, still in great poverty, under the care of a housekeeper. But the father's vice grew upon him until Beethoven, at the age of eighteen, had to assume full responsibility. As the result of a petition from Beethoven to the Elector the father's services were wholly dispensed with, and half his salary was taken from him and paid to the son. At this time, therefore, Beethoven had assumed the full duties of a man.

So far, Beethoven's education in the less desirable aspects of life had been pretty thorough; he had learned lessons he never forgot. Even in his earliest compositions there are indications of an experience of suffering altogether unusual in so young a boy. Later on, when Beethoven was exulting in his consciousness of his own tremendous power, this element in his music underwent a curious and temporary transformation. But at this time Beethoven could still have doubts about the precise worth of his musical capacity. Bonn offered him no proper outlet for his energies, his home life was hardly stimulating, and he probably became more and more aware of his lack of general culture. The general culture of his time consisted chiefly in the idealization of certain characters in Latin and Greek literature. It was the kind of thing that could be picked up quite readily by conversation and by reading a few translations. "A life-long love of the ancient classics," especially on the part of the nobility, was sufficiently witnessed to by a certain readiness in quoting "lofty" sentiments. For what it was worth Beethoven, about this time, acquired this culture by becoming a constant visitor at the house of the wealthy and cultured von Breuning family. Intercourse with these amiable people, excursions and holidays with them in the country, gave him much happiness. At the same period the Elector established a theatrical orchestra, besides that belonging to the Court Chapel, and Beethoven became a viola player in both. The theatrical orchestra, directed by Joseph Reicha, consisted of very good performers, and during the four years that Beethoven was associated with it, it played a large number of the most famous operas of almost every well-known school of composition. Beethoven thus had first-class opportunities of gaining experience of instrumental music. And a band of wood-wind players, that the Elector probably brought with him from Vienna, would seem to have given Beethoven his quite unusual insight into the possibilities of these instruments. Besides this, a summer expedition with the orchestra up the Rhine gave Beethoven his first opportunity of comparing himself with a great pianist. This pianist was the Abbé Sterkel. He excelled in "ladylike" playing, and he sufficiently impressed Beethoven to make the latter reluctant to play after him. The four years from 1788–92 were thus a period of considerable educational activity. The serious part of this education was, of course, the musical part. Although neither in pianoforte playing nor in composition was Beethoven ever docile enough to model himself upon a master, he was receptive enough to learn whatever he wanted to learn. His criticism, as is always the case with a creative genius, was with reference to his own needs. What he learned depended not only on what he was taught, but on what he felt ministered to his own musical growth.

The same is true of what general culture he imbibed. There was very little in the current education that he could have assimilated, even if he had had the opportunity. Ideas and information, for their own sake, never interested Beethoven. He could absorb nothing, in fact, he could understand nothing, that he could not make a living, organic part of himself. Amongst the lofty sentiments of the ancients and of Goethe he found some that he could interpret as principles in which he believed, and he was never tired of reading them. But his way of regarding literature was utterly different from that of the ordinary educated man or literary connoisseur. He lacked the necessary detachment. For that reason he blamed Mozart for composing music to licentious librettos. He was altogether too much convinced of the overwhelming importance of good and evil to take up an "art for art's sake" attitude.

CHAPTER TWO

The Morality of Power

BY NOVEMBER, 1792, when Beethoven left Bonn for Vienna, his development, from every point of view, was considerable. His circumstances, combined with his intense and responsive nature, had given him an outlook on life that was thoroughly mature. He knew poverty, suffering, and responsibility. He had also acquired a very respectable standing as an artist. Not only his fellow professional musicians, but his cultured friends, amongst whom was Count Waldstein, entertained high hopes of his future. Joseph Haydn, on his passage through Bonn, had been very favourably impressed with one of his cantatas. As a pianist he was already famous. He had every reason to hope that he could make a career for himself in the great world.

It is impossible to know how early a genius of the Beethoven order is conscious of his own powers. The feeling that one is extraordinary and destined to future greatness does not seem to be confined to extraordinary

58

people, and it is probable that not all extraordinary people have it. Beethoven's achievements were already considerable, and it is probable that he valued them highly. But he lacked what he would have considered satisfactory evidence that they justified the highest ambitions. His fame in Bonn was, after all, a local fame. We must assume, if not a self-distrust, at least a certain caution in Beethoven's attitude at this time. This would explain why he went to Vienna as a student, and also his outbursts of arrogant self-confidence when he found he could pass all the tests. His studies with Haydn, Schenk, Albrechtsberger and Salieri, seem to have been undertaken with the idea of finding out if there really was anything of value in the rules they had to teach him. It is the attitude of a man too little confident or too much in earnest to neglect even the most unpromising material. Musical theorists assure us that these studies were valuable to Beethoven, but his own references to them do not bear out this assertion. Nevertheless, it was several months before he made up his mind that he had nothing to learn that these men could teach. Even while studying their rules he resented any strictures based on the application of them to his compositions. He would do the exercises in the hope that the discipline or some other mysterious quality attending the performance would prove of advantage to him, but when it came to the actual composition of music then, as Thayer says: "Beethoven the composer stood upon his own territory, followed his own tastes and impulses, wrote and wrought subject to no other control." At this period of his life Beethoven, as is natural with a young, earnest and uneducated man, was submissive before cultural mysteries, albeit with bursts of impatience and defiance. But when it came to something he understood, such as actual music as distinct from learned theories about it, his judgment was instant, decisive, and independent. Thus, when his three trios, Op. 1, were first introduced to the musical world at a soirée at Prince Lichnowsky's, everyone eagerly awaited Haydn's opinion. That opinion was unfavourable to the third trio, the one in C minor, but this, so far from shaking Beethoven's opinion that it was the best of the three, merely convinced him that Haydn was actuated by envy, jealousy and malice. That his own musical judgment should be wrong, even about his own compositions, seems to have been inconceivable to him, and he could not understand that anyone not a fool could honestly disagree with him. But, outside music, Beethoven manifested no such consciousness of infallible insight. In literature, for instance, he seems largely to have accepted current estimates.

Any doubts that he may have brought with him to Vienna concerning the precise extent of his musical abilities speedily vanished. He very rapidly became a great success, both as a pianist and, later, as a composer. Sponsored by Count Waldstein, and already known to many prominent men, he mixed freely with the highest society in Vienna. He found that he could do this without making any concessions. He had merely to be himself. The force that dwelt in him was immediately and unquestioningly recognized, and was tacitly accepted as more than sufficient to obliterate what differences of rank and culture there might be. Only a little before even a Mozart and Haydn were ranked as servants of the nobility. Beethoven was never on this footing. The difference must have been due wholly to his force of character. His compositions did not, at this time, entitle him to rank with Mozart or even Haydn, so that the attitude of the Viennese nobility towards him was not due to a belated recognition on their part of the reverence due to genius. His great powers as a pianist doubtless made him acceptable to the music-loving Viennese aristocracy, but there was nothing of the diplomatic deference of the performing poodle, an attitude to which many good men had been compelled, in Beethoven's relations with them. The few attempts that were made to treat him *de haut en bas* were immediately and very effectively resented. His behaviour seems to have been entirely free from nervousness, deference, or constraint. He showed himself perfectly fearless in his public contests with other pianists, and his victories—sometimes annihilating ones —seem to have been only what he expected. Beethoven's success must have had the effect of strengthening his conviction that his force was equal to any demands that might be made upon it. He denied himself nothing; he gave every impulse its free vent. He cheerfully made enemies amongst his rivals. He took no pains to humour his patrons. He spent his money, if not recklessly, at least carelessly. It was as if, in spite of his early glimpses of the dark side of life, he was now convinced that his sheer strength was sufficient to protect him from all ill. This was partly due, of course, to the intoxicating realization of his own genius. People already saw in him a second Mozart, and Beethoven, we may be sure, felt that he was destined to something even greater. And Beethoven at this time greatly desired fame. His genius was to be exploited for his personal glory. He had not yet reached the position of seeing himself rather as a priest than as a king. His general attitude is exhibited in one of his arrogantly humorous letters to Court Secretary Von Zmeskall. "The devil take you," he says, "I don't want to know anything about your whole system of ethics. *Power* is the morality of men who stand out from the rest, and it is also mine."

But it would be a mistake to suppose that Beethoven was a young genius whose success had gone to his head. He really was a strong man. His consciousness of power was not merely the reflection of other people's opinions about him. He has none of the strained air of a man who is wilfully maintaining an attitude. Directly something important, such as the feelings of an old friend, are involved, away goes all the youthful Beethoven's cynicism and arrogance. It never occurs to him that he has a pose to maintain, simply because he had not been maintaining a pose. His letter to Wegeler, written between 1794 and 1796, shows how perfectly sound was his sense of values.

> "My dearest, my best one!
>
> "What a horrid picture you have drawn to me of myself! I recognize it, I do not deserve your friendship. You are so noble, so kindly disposed, and now for the first time I do not dare to compare myself with you; I have fallen far below you. Alas! for weeks I have given pain to my best, my noblest friend. You believe I have ceased to be kind-hearted, but, thank Heaven, 'tis not so. It was not intentional, thought-out malice on my part, which caused me to act thus; but my unpardonable thoughtlessness, which prevented me from seeing the matter in the

right light. I am thoroughly ashamed for your sake, also for mine. I scarcely venture to beg you to restore your friendship. Ah! Wegeler, my only consolation is that you knew me almost from my childhood, and—oh, let me say it myself—I was really always of good disposition, and in my dealings always strove to be upright and honest; how, otherwise, could you have loved me! Could I, then, in so short a time have suddenly changed so terribly, so greatly to my disadvantage? Impossible that these feelings for what is great and good should all of a sudden become extinct. My Wegeler, dear and best one, venture once again to come to the arms of your B. Trust to the good qualities which you formerly found in him, I will vouch for it that the pure temple of holy friendship which you will erect on it will for ever stand firm; no chance event, no storm will be able to shake its foundations—firm —eternal—our friendship—forgiveness—forgetting —revival of dying, sinking friendship. Oh, Wegeler! do not cast off this hand of reconciliation; place your hand in mine—O God!—but no more—I myself come to you and throw myself in your arms, and sue for the lost friend, and you will give yourself to me full of contrition, who loves and ever will be mindful of you."

We do not know what particular manifestation of "power" was followed by this repentance, but Beethoven found, during this period, that his philosophy of power was, on the whole, successful. It had not been very severely tested. The death of his father, towards the end of 1792, could not have distressed him very greatly, and he assumed the extra share of responsibility for his brothers with equanimity. In 1795 he proposed marriage to a former Bonn colleague, Magdalena Willman, now famous in Vienna as a singer, but her refusal does not seem to have given him much concern. Being a really strong man Beethoven could never have taken his morality of power with the seriousness of a Nietzsche. His ideal was the hero, not the strong man. But strength cannot become heroism until the soul has known despair, and just now Beethoven found everything easy. He became careless and forgot to fear God or his fellow-men. His overbearing manners, about which we have evidence even when he was known merely as a pianist, were not those of an uncouth provincial, misbehaving himself in all innocence. They were the expression of one of Beethoven's most lasting characteristics, a profound contempt for the great bulk of his fellow-men. This contempt was by no means always savage; it was often robustly good-humoured. But there can be no question but that it was there. It was perfectly compatible with that love for humanity he afterwards professed, for that love was based on the vision that came to him of humanity as a suffering humanity. But all his life he had the contempt of *"eine Natur"* for the *"süsse Puppe."* To such a man the majority of human beings are more or less random collections of borrowed emotions and borrowed ideas. They are, to an extent he finds it difficult to understand, the result of their accidental circumstances. He feels in them an entire absence of the integrating strength and courage that dwells in himself. Their culture and morality, their aims in life, even their joys and sorrows, seem to him merely characterless reflections of their environment. They have none of his passion for heroic achievement, and in any case they would be incapable of paying the price for it. They are never honest, for the last thing they would face is themselves in their essential loneliness. With such creatures a man of Beethoven's kind could never be really intimate. He could treat them with rough good-humour or, if they offended him, he could blaze out in contemptuous wrath. But he could never treat them with the consideration and respect that a man shows towards his equals. He could hurt their feelings with careless indifference, believing that their feelings were of no consequence even if they really existed. The only attitude a *"süsse Puppe"* can take up towards such a man is either one of admiration or one of hatred. Beethoven had plenty of enemies who could not forget the wounds to their vanity that he had inflicted. But also, besides the men he genuinely respected, he had plenty of friends who put up with his contemptuous lack of restraint. At times he tried to be coldly diplomatic with people and to conceal from them the contempt he felt. Thus, he notes in the 1814 diary: "Never show to men the contempt they deserve, one never knows to what use one may want to put them." Even during the early years in Vienna he adopted this diplomatic attitude. Thus, speaking of men who doubtless considered themselves his intimate friends, he describes one as "too weak for friendship" and goes on: "I consider him and . . . mere instruments on which, when it pleases me, I play; but they can never become noble witnesses of my inner and outer activity, nor be in true sympathy with me; I value them according as they are useful to me." Usually, however, he felt no need of such restraint. Even for so considerable a genius as

Haydn he did not conceal a certain sneering condescension. Smaller men had to endure being tossed up and down as the mood took him. Two letters to the composer J. N. Hummel, on two consecutive days, run as follows:

> "Do not come to me any more. You are a false fellow, and the knacker take all such."

.

> "Good friend Nazerl,
> "You are an honourable fellow, and I see you were right. So come this afternoon to me. You will also find Schuppanzigh, and both of us will bump, thump and pump you to your heart's delight."

His relations with most of his fellow-men remained at this stage throughout his life. His rapid alternations of feeling for one and the same person are often comic, and seem to testify to a complete lack of insight on his part. But his apparent lack of "human understanding" is due to the lack of anything there he particularly wanted to understand. He was, almost more than any man that ever lived, *"eine Natur,"* and the *"süsse Puppes"* never seemed to him to be real people at all. Even Goethe found this attitude in him a little disconcerting, as he complains in a letter to Zelter. "His talent amazed me; unfortunately he is an utterly untamed personality, not altogether in the wrong in holding the world to be detestable, but who does not make it any the more enjoyable either for himself or for others by his attitude." Even Goethe found Beethoven excessive, although he understood the attitude. He had earlier written: "A more self-contained, energetic, sincere artist I never saw. I can understand right well how singular must be his attitude towards the world."

But this attitude was complicated by the very quick and rich emotional nature he possessed. Beethoven, especially at this time, was no misanthrope. The whole man was intensely alive and lived in a vivid world. Everything interested him. He was eager for society, and for anything that contributed to the wealth of impressions that poured in upon him every day. His art was not yet a refuge to him, a mystery to be served, the only region in which his soul could escape all trammels and become completely free, but a glorious vehicle for the expression of the vivid experiences life presented to him. He enjoyed conversation and reading, brilliant social functions, and unconstrained laughter in taverns. He travelled. And, at this time, according to Wegeler, he was always in love, "and made many conquests which would have been difficult if not impossible for many an Adonis." All this made an excellent setting for the morality of power. Beethoven's real strength, his contempt for others, and his success, must have made this doctrine thoroughly congenial to him. He was, in fact, admirably constructed to be an exponent of the morality of power. But a higher destiny was reserved for him.

It would appear that Beethoven first noticed symptoms of his deafness in 1798. His first reference to it, however, occurs in a letter to Amenda, dated June 1, 1801. The letter is most interesting as showing us Beethoven's attitude, at this time, towards the impending calamity. His first reaction, as we should expect, is rage at the *senselessness* of the hideous affliction. That he, of all men, should lose this particular sense must, indeed, have seemed the most abominable of ironies.

> "Your Beethoven is most unhappy," he writes, "and at strife with nature and Creator. I have often cursed the latter for exposing his creatures to the merest accident, so that often the most beautiful buds are broken or destroyed thereby. Only think that my noblest faculty, my hearing, has greatly deteriorated."

But still he has hopes, although he fears the worst, and his self-confidence remains indomitable.

> ". . . it is said to be due to my bowels and so far as they are concerned I am nearly restored to health. I hope, indeed, that my hearing will also improve, but I am dubious, because such diseases are the most incurable. How sad is my lot! I must avoid all things that are dear to me and live amongst such miserable and egotistical men as . . . and . . . and others. I must say that amongst them all Lichnowsky is the most satisfactory, since last year he has settled an income of 600 florins on me and the good sale of my works enables me to live without care. I could sell everything I compose five times over and at a good price. . . . Oh, how happy could I be if my hearing were completely restored; then would I hurry to you, but as it is I must refrain from everything and the most beautiful years of my life must pass without accomplishing the promise of my talent and powers. A sad resignation to which I must resort although, indeed, I am resolved to rise superior to every obstacle. But how will that be possible? . . . My affliction causes me the least trouble in playing and composing, the most in asso-

ciation with others, and you must be my companion. I am sure my fortune will not desert me. With whom need I be afraid of measuring my strength? Since you have been gone I have composed every sort of music except operas and church music. . . . I beg of you to keep the matter of my deafness a profound secret to *be confided to nobody no matter who it is.* . . ."

In a letter to his doctor friend Wegeler, written at the end of the same month, he goes more into detail.

". . . my hearing has grown steadily worse for three years for which my bowels, which you know were always wretched and have been getting worse, since I am always troubled with a dysentery, in addition to unusual weakness, are said to be responsible. Frank wanted to tone up my body by tonic medicines and restore my hearing with almond oil, but, *prosit,* nothing came of the effort; my hearing grew worse and worse, and my bowels remained as they had been. This lasted till the autumn of last year, and I was often in despair. Then came a medical ass who advised me to take cold baths, a more sensible one to take the usual lukewarm Danube bath. That worked wonders; my bowels improved, my hearing remained, or became worse. I was really miserable during this winter; I had frightful attacks of colic and I fell back into my previous condition, and so things remained until about four weeks ago, when I went to Vering, thinking that my condition demanded a surgeon, and having great confidence in him. He succeeded almost wholly in stopping the awful diarrhœa. He prescribed the lukewarm Danube bath, into which I had each time to pour a little bottle of strengthening stuff, gave me no medicine of any kind until about four weeks ago, when he prescribed pills for my stomach and a kind of tea for my ear. Since then I can say I am stronger and better; only my ears whistle and buzz continually, day and night. I can say I am living a wretched life; for two years I have avoided almost all social gatherings because it is impossible for me to say to people: 'I am deaf.' If I belonged to any other profession it would be easier, but in my profession it is an awful state, the more since my enemies, who are not few, what would they say? In order to give you an idea of this singular deafness of mine I must tell you that in the theatre I must get very close to the orchestra in order to understand the actor. If I am a little distant I do not hear the high tones of the instruments, singers, and if I be put a little farther away I do not here at all. Frequently I can hear the tones of a low conversation, but not the words, and as soon as anybody shouts it is intolerable. It seems singular that in conversation there are people who do not notice my condition at all, attributing it to my absent-mindedness. Heaven knows what will happen to me. *Vering says that there will be an improvement if no complete cure.* I have often—cursed my existence. *Plutarch* taught me resignation. If possible I will bid defiance to my fate, although there will be moments in my life when I shall be the unhappiest of God's creatures. . . . Resignation! What a wretched refuge—and yet the only one open to me. . . ."

In November he again writes to Wegeler. His hearing has become no better, but rather worse. The slight hope of improvement that he had seems to have abandoned him, so that now he clutches eagerly at any chance. He thinks of changing his physician, accusing Vering of negligence. And he has been collecting stories of marvellous cures. "Miracles are told of *galvanism;* what have you to say about it? A doctor told me that he had seen a deaf and dumb child recover his hearing (in Berlin) again—and a man who had been deaf 7 years got well."

Then comes a reference to *"a dear, fascinating girl* who loves me and whom I love. There have been a few blessed moments within the last two years and it is the first time that I feel marriage might bring me happiness. Alas! she is not of my station—and now—it would be impossible for me to marry, I must still hustle about actively." It is highly probable that the "dear fascinating girl" referred to was the Countess Julia Guicciardi, at the date of this letter just one week less than seventeen years of age. But there is no convincing evidence that she ever played any important part in Beethoven's life. And it does not appear that the impossibility of marriage to which he refers was in any way due to his affliction. But doubtless the general exaltation produced by "being in love" intensified Beethoven's perceptions of the desirability of those aspects of life that his deafness was making inaccessible to him.

> "Oh, if I were rid of this affliction I could embrace the world! I feel that my youth is just beginning and have I not always been ill? My physical strength has for a short time past been steadily growing more than ever and also my mental powers. Day by day I am approaching the goal which I apprehend but cannot describe. It is

only in this that your Beethoven can live. Tell me nothing of rest. I know of none but sleep, and woe is me that I must give up more time to it than usual. Grant me but half freedom from my affliction and then—as a complete, ripe man I shall return to you and renew the old feelings of friendship. You must see me as happy as it is possible to be here below—not unhappy. No! I cannot endure it. I will take Fate by the throat; it shall not wholly overcome me. Oh, it is so beautiful to live—to live a thousand times! I feel that I am not made for a quiet life."

During the winter of 1801–2 Beethoven did change his physician, the new one being Dr. Schmidt, and on his advice spent the summer of 1802 at the near but quiet and secluded village of Heiligenstadt. Schmidt seems to have given Beethoven hopes that the quiet, by lessening the demands on his hearing, would effect an improvement. Up till now, as we see quite clearly from the letters, Beethoven's reaction to the impending calamity was defiance. He felt that he must assert his will in order not to be overcome. He would summon up all his strength in order to go on living and working in spite of his fate. "I will take Fate by the throat." He was, as it were, *defending* his creative power. But by the end of this summer he found that his genius, that he had felt called upon to cherish and protect, was really a mighty force using him as a channel or servant. It is probable that every genius of the first order becomes aware of this curious relation towards his own genius. Even the most fully conscious type of genius, the scientific genius, as Clerk Maxwell and Einstein, reveals this feeling of being *possessed.* A power seizes them of which they are not normally aware except by obscure premonitions. With Beethoven, so extraordinarily creative, a state of more or less unconscious tumult must have been constant. But only when the consciously defiant Beethoven had succumbed, only when his pride and strength had been so reduced that he was willing, even eager, to die and abandon the struggle, did he find that his creative power was indeed indestructible and that it was its deathless energy that made it impossible for him to die. This new and profound realization of his nature is the most significant thing in the famous Heiligenstadt Testament, written in the autumn of this year, but not discovered till after his death. It marks the complete collapse of the old morality of power, and shows the experiences that made possible the erection of a new morality of power on the ruins of the old. The document must be quoted in full.

For my brothers Carl and—Beethoven

O ye men who think or say that I am malevolent, stubborn or misanthropic, how greatly do ye wrong me, you do not know the secret causes of my seeming, from childhood my heart and mind were disposed to the gentle feelings of good will, I was even ever eager to accomplish great deeds, but reflect now that for 6 years I have been in a hopeless case, aggravated by senseless physicians, cheated year after year in the hope of improvement, finally compelled to face the prospect of a *lasting malady* (whose cure will take years or, perhaps, be impossible), born with an ardent and lively temperament, even susceptible to the diversions of society,

73

I was compelled early to isolate myself, to live in loneliness, when I at times tried to forget all this, O how harshly was I repulsed by the doubly sad experience of my bad hearing, and yet it was impossible for me to say to men speak louder, shout, for I am deaf. Ah how could I possibly admit an infirmity in the one sense which should have been more perfect in me than in others, a sense which I once possessed in highest perfection, a perfection such as few surely in my profession enjoy or ever have enjoyed—O I cannot do it, therefore forgive me when you see me draw back when I would gladly mingle with you, my misfortune is doubly painful because it must lead to my being misunderstood, for me there can be no recreation in society of my fellows, refined intercourse, mutual exchange of thought, only just as little as the greatest needs command may I mix with society. I must live like an exile, if I approach near to people a hot terror seizes upon me, a fear that I may be subjected to the danger of letting my condititon be observed—thus it has been during the last year which I spent in the country, commanded by my intelligent physician to spare my hearing as much as possible, in this almost meeting my present natural disposition, although I sometimes ran counter to it yielding to my inclination for society, but what a humiliation when one stood beside me and heard a flute in the distance and *I heard nothing,* or someone heard *the shepherd singing* and again I heard nothing, such incidents brought me to the verge of despair, but little more and I would have put an end to my life—only art it was that withheld me, ah it seemed impossible to leave the world until I had produced all that I felt called upon to produce, and so I endured this wretched existence —truly wretched, an excitable body which a sudden change can throw from the best into the worst state—Patience—it is said I must now choose for my guide, I have done so, I hope my determination will remain firm to endure until it pleases the inexorable parcæ to break the thread, perhaps I shall get better, perhaps not, I am prepared. Forced already in my 28th year to become a philosopher, O it is not easy, less easy for the artist than for anyone else—Divine One thou lookest into my inmost soul, thou knowest it, thou knowest that love of man and desire to do good live therein. O men, when some day you read these words, reflect that ye did me wrong and let the unfortunate one comfort himself and find one of his kind who despite all the obstacles of nature yet did all that was in his power to be accepted among worthy artists and men. You my brothers Carl and   as soon as I am dead if Dr. Schmid is still alive ask him in my name to describe my malady and attach this document to the history of my illness so that so far as possible at least the world may become reconciled with me after my death. At the same time I declare you two to be the heirs to my small fortune (if so it can be called), divide it fairly, bear with and help each other, what injury you have done me you know was long ago forgiven. To you brother Carl I give special thanks for the attachment you have displayed towards me of late. It is my wish that your lives may be better and freer from care than I have had, recommend virtue to your children, it alone can give happiness, not money, I speak from experience, it was virtue that upheld me in misery, to it next to my art I owe the fact that I did not end my life by suicide.—Farewell and love each other—I thank all my friends, particularly *Prince Lichnowsky* and *Professor Schmid*—I desire that the instruments from Prince L. be preserved by one of you but let no quarrel result from this, so soon as they can serve you a better purpose sell them, how glad will I be if I can still be helpful to you in my grave—with joy I hasten towards death—if it comes before I shall have had an opportunity to show all my artistic capacities it will still come too early for me despite my hard fate and I shall probably wish that it had come later—but even then I am satisfied, will it not free me from a state of endless suffering? Come when thou will I shall meet thee bravely.—Farewell and do not wholly forget me when I am dead, I deserve this of you in having often in life thought of you how to make you happy, be so—

LUDWIG VAN BEETHOVEN.

[Seal.]

Heiglnstadt,
October 6th, 1802.

For my brothers Carl and   to be read and executed after my death.

Heiglnstadt, October 10th, 1802, thus do I take my farewell of thee—and indeed sadly—yes that beloved hope—which I brought with me when I came here to be cured at least in a degree—I must wholly abandon, as the leaves of autmun fall and are withered so hope has been blighted, almost as I came—I go away—even the high courage—which

often inspired me in the beautiful days of summer
—has disappeared—O Providence—grant me at last
but one day of pure joy—it is so long since real
joy echoed in my heart—O when—O when, O
Divine One—shall I find it again in the temple of
nature and of men—Never? no—O that would be
too hard.

This document marks a crisis in Beethoven's life.
Never again was his attitude towards life one of defiance,
where the defiance was an expression of what is called
his "strength of character." He had no such need of defiance, for he no longer had any fear. He had become
aware within himself of an indomitable creative energy
that nothing could destroy. It is this realization, become
exultant, that makes him break off in sketching the
theme of the great C major fugue of the third Rasou-
mowsky quartet to write in the margin that nothing can
now hinder his composing: "In the same way that you
are now able to throw yourself into the whirlpool of society, so you are able to write your works in spite of all
social hindrances. Let your deafness no longer be a secret
—even for art." He is no longer afraid for his art. He
no longer fears that "the most beautiful years of my life
must pass without accomplishing the promise of my talent and powers." And to this consciousness of indomitable creative power, the deepest thing in Beethoven, he
continually gives expression in his music. The quartet
fugue just mentioned is such an expression, although
an even more irresistible manifestation of sheer force is
to be found in the Scherzo of the ninth symphony.
Such movements are in no sense programme music, although they may form a part of a programmatic whole.

Such music expresses qualities, not experiences. The quality that survived the experience depicted in the first movement of the ninth symphony and enabled the composer to achieve the state depicted in the third movement was precisely the primitive unconquerable energy depicted in the Scherzo. This quality was the most primitive and most lasting thing in Beethoven. It is almost symbolic that his last recorded action, when lying unconscious on his death-bed, should have been the shaking of his fist towards heaven in response to a shattering peal of thunder.

His realization of the deep-rooted character of his own creative power, which we date from the Heiligenstadt Testament, changed the character of the problem of his attitude towards life. A rigid, strained defiance was no longer necessary. What he came to see as his most urgent task, for his future spiritual development, was *submission*. He had to learn to accept his suffering as in some mysterious way necessary.

CHAPTER THREE

The Mind of Beethoven

THE HEILIGENSTADT TESTAMENT was very carefully written and copied by Beethoven, yet even here he is not wholly articulate. Such phrases as "until it pleases the inexorable parcæ to break the thread," and "as the leaves of autumn fall and are withered so hope has been blighted," have a "literary" note which sounds false in the stammering sincerity of the rest of the document. Yet it is perfectly obvious that the use of these phrases indicates no insincerity whatever; Beethoven was not attitudinizing. His perceptions, where language were concerned, were coarse. He was, where words were concerned, too unsophisticated to detect the cliché or the hollow reverberation of the merely orotund phrase. Language, so far as he was sensitive to it, was a deficient means of expression. Provided he could seize, under this baffling dress of words, a sentiment of which he approved, he was as likely as not to adopt the phrase *en bloc.* The references, in his letters, to the heroes of Greek and Latin mythology, have the same *naïveté*. The names of Bacchus, Hercules, and the rest of them, had not for him the flat, trite, artificial associations they have for the ordinary sophisticated reader. To Beethoven these names stood for vivid and energetic embodiments of life's fundamental forces and principles. Vague and lofty phrases had a better chance of securing Beethoven's attention than had the exquisite and perfect expression of some small idea or unimportant experience, simply because the very vagueness of such phrases enabled him to attribute his own wealth of meaning to them. In his letters Beethoven is often incoherent. He never mastered the grammatical forms of his mother tongue, and even his spelling is poor. In a letter to Wegeler, apologizing for delay in answering a letter he says: "I often compose the answer in my mind, but when I wish to write it down, I usually throw the pen away, because I cannot write as I feel."

No reader of Beethoven's letters can doubt that he was exceptionally insensitive to language as an instrument for the expression of his thoughts and feelings. They give no evidence of a clear, orderly and powerful mind. In this they present so complete a contrast to his music that one is tempted to regard Beethoven as a striking example of the "unconscious" genius. And the stories we have testifying to his "hallucinated" condition when inspired by some musical idea, seem to bear out this theory. The normal Beethoven, this theory would require us to suppose, was not aware of the states of consciousness revealed in his music. Such states did not enter into his fully conscious mind. The serenity of the slow movement of the ninth symphony, for example, a serenity which contains within itself the deepest and most unforgettable sorrow, and yet a sorrow which is transformed by its inclusion in that serenity; the still more indescribable synthesis expressed in the *Heiliger Dankgesang* of the A minor quartet; these states, we are required to believe, did not form part of the conscious life of Beethoven. They were related to that conscious life no more closely than was the exquisite humour of some of his scherzos with the crude jokes of his everyday life. This theory derives a good deal of what plausibility it has from the fact, that we have already noted, that Beethoven was exceptionally insensitive to language. Many musicians have noticed a peculiar and unique "musicality" about Beethoven. He has been described as "*the* musician who felt, thought, and dreamt in tones." It is difficult for the ordinary man, who is always predominantly a word-user, to understand that to Beethoven language was a clumsy device for communication, that to him music was an altogether more natural, subtle, and adequate means of expression. That it was so is due to the fact that what Beethoven wanted to express did not belong to that "universe of discourse" with which language primarily deals. We have already noted that he was not particularly interested in ideas. All that world of thought that can be expressed, and expressed only, by propositions, was of no great interest to Beethoven. He could not, it is true, convey in music a request to Frau Nannette Streicher to mend his socks, and he employed language for that purpose. But he employed language for very little but such purposes. Beethoven has sometimes been called a philosophical musician, but if that means that he was a philosopher it is certainly untrue. Music can no more express philosophic ideas than it can express scientific ideas. And nothing that Beethoven wanted to express can be called a philosophy. The states of consciousness he expresses, his reactions to perceptions and experiences, are not ideas. Belief in a Heavenly Father cannot be expressed in music; what can be expressed, and with unexampled power, is the state of soul that such a belief, sincerely held, may arouse. The music of the Credo of Beethoven's Mass in D is not the musical interpretation of certain Latin propositions. The Latin propositions express beliefs; the music expresses states of the soul that may, in some cases, be aroused by those beliefs. Beethoven was not interested in ideas for their own sake—as affording an intellectual, *detached* view of life, a view aiding understanding and prophecy —but only for the states of the soul to which they testified. Thus, when he is excited about "steam cannons," it is not because he is interested in this startling advance in the mechanism of cannons, but because he thinks that they form one more witness to the expanding, energetic, and unconquerable spirit of man. Similarly his interest in Newton's picture of the solar system is due to his exultant realization of the existence of a tremendous and universal force in Nature. In some vague way he felt that this was another embodiment of a quality he so greatly prized in mankind. The fact that the force varied as the inverse square of the distance was not of the slightest interest to him, and it is doubtful whether he would even have understood it. To Beethoven ideas were primarily clues to an attitude towards life on the part of the man who enunciated them. To the "world of ideas," pure and simple, he was a stranger. Pure and simple ideas, "abstract" ideas, reveal an atti-

82

tude towards life only indirectly, and it was the attitude towards life that interested Beethoven. It is entirely typical that, when a young man in Vienna, he refused, although strongly urged, to attend a lecture on Kant. Before deciding, therefore, on the evidence of his letters and reported conversations, that Beethoven was an unconscious genius, we must remember that he was, to an altogether unusual extent, without the "language mentality." It is not only that he was untrained and clumsy in the use of language; his most important states of consciousness, what he would have called his "thoughts," were not of the kind that can be expressed in language. It is probable that he was not wholly aware of the reason why language was to him so refractory a medium. He probably regarded himself as merely clumsy. As he says in a letter to Amalie Sebald, "If I could give as definite expression to my thoughts about my illness as to my thoughts in music, I would soon help myself." The poetic, as distinguished from the propositional use of language, was, of course, much more congenial to him. The state of consciousness communicated by a poem is very seldom an idea that can be expressed in propositional form. Yet even here Beethoven had the greatest difficulty in finding his own states of consciousness rendered in language, as his long and fruitless search for a suitable libretto clearly shows. He wanted a poem that was the product of a state of awareness akin to his own, and he never found it. We may suppose that the reason lay not only in the rarity of great poets but also in probable profound difference between the essentially musical and the essentially linguistic mind. We must admit, in short, that music is not only an independent means of expression, but that its total range of expression is different from that of language. It is more limited than language in the fact that it cannot express ideas at all; it is also possible that there are certain poetic experiences that cannot be expressed in music. But it must also be admitted that it can express states of consciousness that language is not fitted to deal with. And Beethoven, to an extent unusual even amongst musicians, was concerned with such states. Wagner, for instance, was much less "purely" musical than Beethoven, not because of any inferiority in using music as his medium, but because his "thoughts" belonged almost wholly to the world of language. Beethoven is one of the very few musicians who can really be compared with a great and profound poet. Yet we feel that Beethoven differs much more from all great and profound poets than they do from one another. So much of what Beethoven expresses is *unique;* nothing like it can be found elsewhere, either in music or poetry. And yet we regard these unique states as fundamental and greatly prize them. It is as if Beethoven is the one voice that has expressed a certain region of the human soul—states of consciousness that we may call musical in the sense that they have been expressed, and perhaps can be expressed, only by music. But this is not to say that they exist in some state of isolation. They are synthetic results of important experiences and perceptions although these particular syntheses can be expressed, it is probable, only in music. The elements of such a synthesis can often be described in language. Indeed, an important duty of a musical critic is to undertake such descriptions. But the synthesis itself is expressible only in music. The elements constitutive of the spiritual content of the *Grosse Fuge*, for example, could conceivably be described more or less exactly in words. But it is surely impossible to imagine the strange and wonderful synthesis there expressed being communicable in any other medium. But whatever a great poet might do, it is clear that a propositional statement of that synthesis would be self-contradictory. It has been called an expression of the reconciliation of Freedom and Necessity, or of Assertion and Submission, but these phrases are mere stammers to a person not already aware of the state of consciousness concerned. But music can, at least temporarily, communicate such indescribable states to those who have never experienced them before.

The fact, therefore, that the mind expressed in Beethoven's letters is not commensurate with the mind expressed in his music is no proof that he was an unconscious genius, except to the extent that all great geniuses have been unconscious. That superior organization of his experiences and perceptions that is effected by a genius is certainly for the most part unconscious. Numberless experiences extending over several years are gradually co-ordinated in the unconscious mind of the artist, and the total synthetic whole finds expression, it may be, on some particular occasion. Even with poetry, which often professes to have its origin in some particular occasion, the poem is never the effect of the particular occasion acting on some kind of *tabula rasa*. The experience of the particular occasion finds its place within a context, although the impact of the experience may have been necessary to bring this context to the surface. A genius may be defined as a man who is exceptionally rich in recoverable contexts. But the formation of these contexts is, for the most part, an unconscious process. A metaphor "occurs" to the poet. A musical phrase "suggests" another. And the irresistible uprising of powerful and extensive contexts may quite well induce an almost trance-like condition. To this extent not only great artists, but great philosophers and men of science, have been unconscious geniuses. Many mathematicians have been subject to trance-like conditions and, on this ground, there is no reason to suppose that Beethoven was more unconscious than Newton. And can we suppose that the philosopher constantly maintains in his daily life the vision of the universe that comes to him in his moments of finest insight? If we add to these considerations the possibility that Beethoven's states of illumination were not expressible in language at all, and certainly not by him, we are left with no evidence that he was an unconscious genius in any extraordinary degree.

CHAPTER FOUR

The Hero

IT IS USUAL to find that the Eroica symphony marks a definite turning-point in Beethoven's music. We believe this point of view to be entirely justified. Beethoven's music, up to the time that he wrote the Heiligenstadt Testament, is chiefly a music that expresses *qualities*. This is probably what many people mean by "pure" music. Such qualities can only be given the roughest of portmanteau names. We can speak of wit, humour, force, dramatic invention, and so on, but such words are but very pitiful attempts to describe the qualities concerned. Both Voltaire and Tom Hood were witty writers, but the quality of the wit is very difficult in the two cases. Music of this kind is the very opposite of programme music. It need make very little, if any, reference to experience. Elegance, neatness, economy, are the sort of terms that can be applied to the productions of an infant prodigy. Music of this kind reveals, as it were, the actual nature of the composer. It reveals the qualities with which he will face life, the qualities that will condition his experience and his presentation of it. In most of Beethoven's early music his experiences of life enter, not as a mastered and synthetic whole, but as moods. He may be sombre, melancholy, gay, or anything else, but these alternations in a composition have no organic connection. We are not, when listening to an early Beethoven quartet, for instance, becoming acquainted with the elements of one unified spiritual experience. Movements could be interchanged or very different ones substituted, without harming the composition. The only criteria that would have to be observed are those of æsthetic variety and unity, that a quick movement should follow the slow movement and so on and, perhaps, that certain key relationships should be preserved. In this his early music resembles the vast bulk of the music written by Haydn and Mozart. There are also, of course, technical resemblances, although too much stress can be laid on them. When we say that music expresses qualities we are not, of course, describing the content of the music any more than, in describing *Candide* as witty, we are describing the content of *Candide*. But the music we are speaking of does not possess what we have called a "spiritual content," although it expresses spiritual qualities. We may liken it to a mathematical memoir which exhibits elegance, inventive power, imagination, and even wit, but which has no "external" reference whatever. Particularly unambiguous examples of this purely qualitative music are to be found in some of Beethoven's early scherzos. Besides music of this kind there is to be found some "composed" music in Beethoven's early work. He said himself, for instance, of the Adagio affetuoso ed appassionato of the early F major quartet, that he had in mind the tomb scene in *Romeo and Juliet*. The creative process involved here is not the same as that of a dramatist who records his reactions to an imagined situation that he has himself invented. It is, on the contrary, the same process as is involved in writing opera music, and is subject to the same danger, the danger of losing the note of authenticity that belongs to the expression of a personal experience. The more usual the experience to be depicted, the more likely to be shared by all men, the more likely, of course, that it can secure an adequate musical representation. Most operas deal with stock emotions and experiences, for that is the ground on which the poet and the composer can be most assured of understanding one another. The parting of lovers is certainly a stock situation, and the young Beethoven could treat it adequately. Such stock situations were present, we may suspect, on more than one occasion in his early work. It is not until we come to the Eroica symphony that we find expressed an experience individual, profoundly realized, and in the main line of Beethoven's spiritual development. The early music expresses individual qualities, individual moods, and the young composer's conceptions of a few stock poetic situations. Incomparably the most important part of this music, for our purpose, is the music expressing qualities, for it cannot be denied that Beethoven's "poetic" conceptions are sometimes unconvincing. The one-time "favourite" Largo of the D major sonata Op. 10, for example, is something less than perfectly direct and sincere. It is "made" music, "composed" music, and is altogether inferior to the purely qualitative first movement. What is meant by calling an emotion romantic or sentimental is excessively difficult to define, but unquestionably there is implied the statement that such an emotion is feigned or unearned. An experience is being pretended to that has not, in fact, been experienced. We object to the sorrows of Werther that they are not genuine sorrows. But the sorrows of Werther may be taken seriously either through inexperience or shallowness. The "religious" music of Wagner's last years can only be ascribed to a shallow religious nature, but the over-portentous expression of "melancholy" in the young Beethoven is due to the fact that he was young enough to take his comparatively superficial emotion seriously. That it is not due to an incapacity for profounder experience is shown, of course, by what he went on to write.

The first piece of music he composed that has a really profound and important spiritual content is the Eroica symphony. Indeed, the difference from the earlier music is so startling that it points to an almost catastrophic change, or extremely rapid acceleration, in his spiritual development. We have found that such a change is witnessed to by the Heiligenstadt Testament, and we shall see that the Eroica symphony is an amazingly realized and co-ordinated expression of the spiritual experiences that underlay that document. The ostensible occasion of the symphony appears to have been the career of Napoleon Bonaparte, but no amount of brooding over Napoleon's career could have given Beethoven his realization of what we may call the life-history of heroic achievement as exemplified in the Eroica. This is obviously a transcription of personal experience. He may have thought Napoleon a hero, but his conception of the heroic he had earned for himself. It has been objected to the symphony that the Funeral March is in the wrong place and that it should follow the Scherzo. But this objection entirely misses the organic connection of the whole work. The most profound experience that Beethoven had yet passed through was when his courage and defiance of his fate had been followed by despair. He was expressing what he knew when he made the courage and heroism of the first movement succeeded by the black night of the second. And he was again speaking of what he knew when he made this to be succeeded by the indomitable uprising of creative energy in the Scherzo. Beethoven was here speaking of what was perhaps the cardinal experience of his life, that when, with all his strength and courage, he had been reduced to despair, that when the conscious strong man had tasted very death, there came this turbulent, irrepressible, deathless creative energy surging up from depths he had not suspected. The whole work is a miraculously realized expression of a supremely important experience, and is justly regarded as a turning-point in Beethoven's music. The last movement is based on what we know to have been Beethoven's "Prometheus" theme. Having survived death and despair the artist turns to creation. By adopting the variation form Beethoven has been able to indicate the variety of achievement that is now open to his "Promethean" energy. The whole work is a most close-knit psychologic unit. Never before in music has so important, manifold, and completely coherent an experience been communicated.

Although the Eroica symphony is based on a profound personal experience Beethoven was not yet able to express a subjective state in music in a perfectly direct manner. Indeed, it was only towards the end of his life, and principally in the late quartets, that his music became the perfectly direct expression of his inner state. The dramatist may use characters and incidents as symbols, as *carriers* of the state of consciousness he wishes to communicate—as Shakespeare obviously does in *Macbeth*—but the musician, although not so bound to the external world, may also achieve a certain degree of "objectification." There are certain musical forms which are recognized vehicles for certain restricted classes of emotions. Of these forms the funeral march is one. In the Funeral March of the Eroica Beethoven expressed a personal experience, but only to the extent that the form could accommodate it. By using the form he did, to some extent, depersonalize his experience. In this expression it becomes vaguer and also broader, being linked up with the general human experience of death and with the general human foreboding of the darkness beyond. The root content of the movement is Beethoven's personal experience of despair, transformed, by the form adopted, into a representation of a vaguer and more general human experience. Thus it might be supposed to represent the death of Napoleon or Abercrombie or Nelson or of anybody else whose characteristics could be supposed to support comparison with those depicted in the first movement. It is for this reason that the Funeral March, magnificent as it is, seems a little too prominent amongst the other movements of the symphony. There is a little too much *display* about it, it is a little too suggestive of some great public occasion. The whole symphony is certainly on extremely bold lines, but the other movements are relatively personal and authentic in a way that the Funeral March is not. It is probable that only the Beethoven of the last quartets could have invented a form that should have embodied his experience directly and yet on a sufficiently large scale. To the young Beethoven, who had not yet attained the profound and utter loyalty to his own experience that characterized the music of his later years, there was also the attraction of "great subjects," the triumphant satisfaction of surpassing all other musicians in the treatment of recognized "lofty" themes. The fact, also, that sketches for the Funeral March go back to a period preceding the Heiligenstadt Testament shows that the form chosen was not dictated wholly by the experience that actually inspires it. We need not imagine that the organic unity of the Eroica symphony, or of any other of his greater compositions, was due to considerations that were consciously present in the mind of Beethoven. In an organic work of art the succession of its constituents is not ordered in accordance with any consciously held criterion. The feeling that a certain sequence is "right" is nearly always due to causes the artist could not analyse. In suggesting that the Eroica symphony, in its content and sequence, is the musical expression of the experiences that underlay the Heiligenstadt Testament, we are not suggesting that Beethoven consciously intended this representation. The initial idea of an "Heroic" symphony may indeed have been suggested by the career of Napoleon or Abercrombie or anybody else, but in the process of creation Beethoven had to fall back upon his inner resources, the product of his qualities and his experiences. And the criterion of rightness he employed in the development of his composition was supplied by the order his experience had taken on in the depths of his mind. As a consequence of his own experience the concept of heroism was related, in his mind, within a certain context, largely unconscious, and the conception could only be realized within this context. This explains why the symphony, which makes so great an impression of organic unity, nevertheless defies all attempts to interpret it as representing any particular hero's career. This difficulty has led a recent writer to suppose that the three great movements represent three entirely different heroes, and that the Scherzo is a sort of intermezzo put where it is, either because Beethoven was timid of further outraging popular taste or because he did not fully perceive the connection of the elements of his own work. Such unconvincing shifts are made necessary merely through attaching too great importance to whatever external occasions may be conjectured to have prompted the work. For works of art of the magnitude that we are considering the external occasion is never more than what psychologists call a "tripper" incident, releasing energies and contexts that have been formed in entire independence of it.

Beethoven preferred the Eroica symphony to the symphony in C minor, a judgment that it would be difficult to substantiate on purely musical grounds. The "programmes" of the two symphonies are not unrelated, but the Eroica, in spite of the Funeral March, is a more intimate expression of the composer's experience. In

Beethoven's outlook on life which, as we have already said, was not philosophic or rational, certain aspects of life had immense importance and became, as it were, personified. Heroism, for him, was not merely a name descriptive of a quality of certain acts, but a sort of principle manifesting itself in life. As a corollary he had a personified idea of Fate. Fate was his name for a personified conception of those characteristics of life that call out the heroic in man. But in this idea of Fate it is something external. The inner state witnessing to its existence is heroism or, it may be, fear. In talking of Fate Beethoven is not talking of an experience, but of something that conditions experience. To that extent his notion of Fate is a construction, not as with his notion of Heroism, an expression of a direct perception. A feeling of the need and importance of the heroic principle persisted in Beethoven up to the end, but his conception of Fate as some kind of personified external menace disappeared. In depicting this menace, as he does in the first movmeent of the C minor symphony, Beethoven is, as it were, at one remove from reality. Beethoven, with his unequalled capacity for being faithful to his experience, would be obscurely aware of this, and it may be that some such feeling was responsible for his preference for the Eroica. In his later years the experience that he thus interprets in terms of heroism and fate, a contest between what we might call an inner and an outer principle, becomes a contest between two inner principles, assertion and submission. Beethoven had realized that these are the true elements involved, and that a synthesis of them is possible. Fate may still be invoked as some sort of theoretical *rationale* of both attitudes, but the conflicting elements are now both located within the soul itself.

The sketches for the first three movements of the C minor symphony go back to the years 1800 and 1801, when Beethoven was summoning up all his resolution to meet the threatening calamity of deafness. And these three movements, in their final form, still express an earlier stage of the experience that inspires the Eroica symphony. We know from his own words—"Thus Fate knocks at the door"—that Beethoven intended the first movement to convey his sense of the implacable might of that external and maleficent power he called Fate. This is that "Creator" he had "often cursed for exposing his creatures to the merest accident." The conception is simple and straightforward. But out of this conception Beethoven has composed a movement which is not only interesting, but one of the most masterly pieces of music in existence. It has not, perhaps, the wealth of invention that we find in the first movement of the Eroica, for there Beethoven is expressing a more complicated complex of emotions, but it is almost unequalled in the impression it gives of inevitable progression. This is one of the very few compositions of which it can be truthfully said that it does not contain an unnecessary bar. Beethoven often presents to us an organic unity containing within itself dramatic contrasts, but in this movement there is one dominating mood from first to last. Even the little oboe solo serves only to heighten the tension. But a more striking example of the way in which the fundamental impelling urge controls the whole work is shown by the almost imperceptible transformation of the contrasting second subject into a headlong rhythmical figure.[1] Beethoven never wrote anything that sounds more "predestined" from beginning to end, and this is partly due to the lack of complication in the underlying conception. At this time in Beethoven's life the issue was simple and clear-cut. But it is characteristic of him that even so he did not conceive fate as the blind, cold, indifferent, impersonal order of the universe, but as an enemy. We do not suggest that Beethoven ever did anything so ridiculous as to conceive Fate as some powerful and malign being, but his emotional reaction, as the C minor symphony proves, was appropriate to such a conception. In the first movement of the ninth symphony his whole conception has undergone a subtle transformation.

The slow movement of the C minor symphony is one of the less satisfactory of Beethoven's compositions. In the symphony it is a mere resting-place, a temporary escape from the questions aroused by the first movement. In this it plays an altogether different part from the slow movement of the Eroica. It seems as if Beethoven, in working up these early sketches, remained faithful to the experiences of that time. The movement indicates nothing more profound than the "few blessed moments" of the letter to Wegeler. The Scherzo, however, is a very different affair. Dreadful apprehension, defiance, a primitive surging energy, enter into this amazing picture of a tortured mind that has almost abandoned hope. That he should be able to make this material run so swiftly and cleanly is the most striking

[1] Cf. Dyson: *The New Music.*

evidence Beethoven had given up to this time of his immense organizing power. It is too usual, in musical criticism, to call consummate pattern weavers "masters of form," but in making the elements of this Scherzo into a perfectly ordered and economic composition Beethoven has shown a mastery of form that it would be difficult to parallel elsewhere. What might easily have been, in other hands, a desperate chaos of sound and fury, is here a lithe, perfectly controlled, and beautifully shaped movement. At the end of this movement Beethoven carries us, by a crescendo rising out of the brooding expectancy created by the wailing violins and the drum taps, straight into the exultant finale. The whole psychological process of transition depicted in the Eroica is here ignored—probably because it **was** depicted in the Eroica.

CHAPTER FIVE

The End of a Period

In the description we have given of the Eroica and C minor symphonies we have ascribed to each of them a pretty definite spiritual content. We have given, in each case, a "programme." We have related these works directly to a definite personal experience of Beethoven's. In our interpretations of these works we have used our knowledge of the circumstances of Beethoven's life and of his reactions to them. But we believe that, even in entire absence of any knowledge of Beethoven's life, some such interpretations would be inevitable, and that they would be justified. The content we have attributed to these works is described in words sufficiently vague. "Heroism," "despair," "exultation," are not very definite terms. They are very much less definite than the actual content of the music. Beethoven's phrases are as individual as the tones of a voice. Two men may enunciate what we should have to describe, in the poverty of language, as the same sentiment, but the very tones of their voice may communicate very different impressions. There are very different compositions that express despair or exultation, and a description in these terms does not distinguish between them. The musical critic must be resigned to these limitations of language, although one of their unfortunate results is to make the same description appear applicable to many very different compositions. Of many of Beethoven's compositions, for instance, all that can be said is that they depict a passionate and vigorous conflict. Music can express a very general state of this kind without specifying the conflicting elements. Such music lends itself to very diverse interpretations, the only essential being that the element of conflict shall be preserved. A generalized expression of this kind is to be found in the so-called Appassionata sonata. The faintly troubled serenity of the second movement might be à propos of many different experiences, and the resolute, energetic character of the first and the stormy character of the last are similarly unrevealing. What is evident is that the conflict has deep roots and is attended with great passion. And the quality and depth of the passion expressed shows that we are dealing with a rich and profound emotional nature. But it would be useless to attempt to fit a definite psychological programme to the work simply because so many could be fitted. This is not true of the Eroica and C minor symphonies. Only amongst the deepest and most important human experiences could we find those great enough to support these two structures. The fact is that at this time Beethoven did not commit his more important thoughts to the piano. The Appassionata sonata is the most important piano composition of this period, but it is altogether less

rich in content than the Eroica symphony. It is possible
that it presupposes the experiences that inspired that
symphony but, if so, it is in a more generalized and remote way, and is not in any sense a deeper realization of
them. For the study of Beethoven's spiritual development it is not particularly significant. But the sonata
could not be missed out in any attempt to realize Beethoven as man and musician. It is an exceedingly characteristic work, and the dark energy it expresses is nowhere else made so apparent. The other great sonata of
this period, the Waldstein sonata, is of almost "purely"
musical interest. It can be played perfectly by a very shallow person, and from our present point of view is of no
importance, for even the qualities it expresses, apart
from specifically musical talent, are of no particular sig
nificance. It is a sonata that will always be more popular
with pianists than with the public.

An intense effort of realization on Beethoven's part
was required to make definite enough for artistic treatment the states of mind depicted in the Eroica and C
minor symphonies. The reason why so many artists, in
treating "great subjects," achieve bombast is precisely
that they are incapable of this intensity of realization.
Their spiritual nature is not sufficiently profound to enable them to realize such experiences in a perfectly genuine and individual manner. They therefore introduce
"calculated" effects, effects which are not related organ-
ically, and which do not, in truth, correspond to anything in their actual realization of their experience.
They hope that these devices will make their emotion
appear more than life-size. Beethoven's immense capacity for realizing such experiences is well illustrated by

the first movements of the Eroica and C minor symphonies. The Scherzo of the C minor symphony must also have required an extraordinary capacity for realization, for the reason that we are here dealing with a complex of elusive, almost "borderland" states of consciousness. Beethoven is unique amongst composers not only for the depth, importance and number of his inner states, but for his power to realize them and to give them unambiguous expression. Without this power of realization he would still have been a vast and impressive chaos, but not what Wagner called him, "a universe." His slow and laborious manner of shaping his themes is doubtless to be accounted for, in part, by this effort of realization. Facility and fluency he had in plenty, as his unrivalled powers of improvisation demonstrate. Beethoven could find plenty of good music in himself without sounding to the depths. But all his greatest compositions are the results of such soundings. At the time when he plumbed deepest he said to Rochlitz, "I dread the beginning of these large works. Once into the work, and it goes." To sound such depths as Beethoven sounded one must not only have the depths but also great integrity and a great feeling of responsibility towards one's art. Not all artists, even of the first rank, have always overcome the "dread" Beethoven mentions. The last movement of Mozart's G minor quintet is surely an instance of such a failure. Mozart paid the price here of the easy victories his amazing genius had brought him.

Beethoven himself did not always plumb the depths. He was not always busy with major problems and the most significant spiritual experiences. Such works as the fourth, sixth and eighth symphonies depict states of mind that require no such intensity of realization. It is significant that they were all written comparatively quickly and that each of them accompanies, as it were, one of his greater works. They are not in the main line of Beethoven's spiritual development. In these works the artist turns aside from his fundamental problems, and enjoys his art "for its own sake." It is as if Beethoven, after each of his great efforts, took a temporary rest. And it is probable that the moods depicted in these works are more characteristic of the everyday Beethoven than those whose complete realization and expression cost him so much effort. At this time of his life Beethoven's existence was, superficially, a happy one. The implication of shallowness involved in the term "superficial" is intended only with reference to the deepest things in Beethoven, those things that, so far from being part of his normal outlook, cost him a great deal of effort fully to realize. A genius of the Beethoven order has not only greater depths but, as it were, more levels of existence than the ordinary man. The transition from the fourth to the fifth symphony is not the transition from one "mood" to another, both equally valid and representative; it is the transition from one level of experience and realization to another; one might say that the transition is vertical, not horizontal. And the third and fifth symphonies are more important than the fourth in the history of Beethoven because it was the deepest things in him that conditioned his development. The greater importance the world has always attributed to the third, fifth, seventh and ninth symphonies compared with the fourth, sixth and eighth, is not because of any purely musical superiority they possess, but because everyone is more or less clearly aware that greater issues are involved, that something more important for mankind is being expressed. That there is a deepening or, at any rate, a changing, spiritual content in Beethoven's work taken in chronological order is very obvious, but it does not follow that this development is uniform or even continuous. Spiritual growth, no more than physical growth, proceeds uniformly. The main stages of Beethoven's development are more clearly reflected in certain works than in others. Corresponding to each stage of growth there are a number of works whose reference to that state is only indirect. The fourth symphony is a composition belonging to this class. Although it is not one of Beethoven's most important compositions it expresses more than a mere mood. It is, in fact, an exquisite realization of a state of mind that was possible to Beethoven for some years, a state of warm human happiness based on a confident and optimistic outlook on life. He was at this time thirty-six years of age, and for a few years yet it was possible for him to contemplate marriage. Romantic love was still an element of experience to which Beethoven felt he had a right. In the slow movement it contributes its part to the sheer joy of existence felt by a sensitive, but strong, confident and healthy man. We need not suppose that any actual love experience inspired the slow movement of this symphony. The state depicted could very well exist without an object. Indeed, there is a certain deliberateness, a sort of formality, about this movement, that suggests a purely imaginative realization of the state depicted. It is the expression of a romantic dream, and in its controlled and shapely loveliness it lacks the poignancy of a definite individual experience. It is again one of those movements in which Beethoven expresses a generalized human experience. The whole symphony strikes one as an extremely conscious piece of work. It is the deliberate recording of a state of joy, craved after and greatly prized, that Beethoven probably never experienced for twelve hours together. It is a record of those moments when the suffering and the struggle could be ignored, when his spirit lightened and expanded and turned upwards towards the sun, when he could believe that his normal heritage as a man would not permanently be withheld from him. There is a rich adult warmth and vigour in this gaiety; it is something very different from the early-morning innocence we sometimes find in Mozart. That Beethoven knew that he was here giving expression to an essentially temporary state is clearly indicated by the adagio introduction. Here is a hint of the mysterious and ominous depths from which his spirit is emerging. The brooding darkness gradually lightens until, with an accelerated rising movement we are borne, on an exhilarating burst, into the full daylight of the first movement. The whole of this passage has all the effect of an escape, not of a victory.

As compared with the string quartet, the symphony is a less intimate means of expression. It is more massive and less subtle. In composing a symphony a composer has a tendency to do both more and less than justice to his actual content. The great must be presented as the gigantic, and the elusive as definite. It gives us the monarch on a great state occasion rather than the man. It is for this reason that the true Beethoven of any period is more accurately reflected in the string quartets than in the symphonies. Beethoven wrote string quartets only with great circumspection and with a very keen sense of responsibility. In these he is more rigorously faithful to his experience, less "dramatic," less "objective," than anywhere else in his music. The string quartet is the most sincere form of musical expression, as the opera is the least. Beethoven wrote one opera, not one of his most successful works, and that at a time when his creative activity, through its very activity and abundance, was not perfectly discriminating. Later, when he was less ebullient and had to undertake the revision of the opera, he said he had earned "a martyr's crown." But he wrote sixteen quartets and during his last and greatest creative period he wrote nothing else. The greater intimacy, the greater *faithfulness,* as it were, of his string quartets is admirably illustrated by the three Rasoumovskys, composed in 1806. At this time, as we have seen, Beethoven's fundamental attitude towards life was based on his realization of the victory that may be achieved by heroism in spite of suffering. He was to exult, for a few years, in the confidence this realization brought him. He thought he had found the key to life. The life-history of this realization is depicted in both the Eroica and the C minor symphonies, although it is only in the last movement of the C minor that the full joy and confidence of the victor is revealed. In the last movement of the Eroica the artist, having passed through the valley of the shadow, is depicted as taking his first look at the new world rather than as entering into it. But in both these works the whole process is objectified. It is "dramatized" and presented on the biggest possible scale. The hero marches forth, indubitably heroic, but performing his feats before the whole of an applauding world. What is he like in his loneliness? We find the answer in the Rasoumovsky quartets.

The opening theme of the first Rasoumovsky quartet has not the dramatic, arresting quality of the Eroica theme, but it is nevertheless "heroic." Its sober resolution is appropriate to a more mundane world than that of the grandiose visions of the Eroica. It conveys a truer impression, we may be sure, of Beethoven's daily spiritual food. Its assurance is less conscious, less wilful. But, except that they have a more intimate and less obviously dramatic quality, the Rasoumovsky quartets are essentially concerned with the psychological process with which we are familiar. This is true, more particularly, of the first and third. The second quartet, in E minor, stands somewhat apart from the others. It suggests that the "Fate" that is to be overcome is not some external menace, some threatening and maleficent power, but Beethoven's own loneliness. The first movement, with its suggestion of an enforced and bitter loneliness, its yearnings, and its outbursts of something very like rage, is one of the greatest and most dramatic movements in this group of quartets. The slow movement of this quartet and the slow movement of the preceding quartet, in F major, are the greatest slow movements that Beethoven wrote at this period. They are magnificent examples of that function that music performs with unequalled subtlety, the function of presenting us with a synthesis of emotions or, as Gurney called them, "fused emotions." The complexity of their effect can be realized if we compare them with such a composition as the slow movement of the C minor symphony, for example. Such fusions are not obtained by contrast. Contrast gives the effect of a psychological transition. The different elements of the music we are discussing are not contrasted, but unified. A more elementary example of such a synthesis is to be found in the broken-winged gaiety of the Allegretto of the E minor quartet. The slow movement of the third Rasoumovsky quartet is not so complex, but the emotion it conveys, although simpler, is much more strange. This movement, indeed, stands alone amongst Beethoven's compositions, and throws an unexpected light upon his imaginative resources. Beethoven's imagination and emotional nature, although so intense, is, on the whole, of a normal kind. Most of the very great artists may be regarded as huge extensions of the normal man, which is the chief reason why they are so valuable. Beethoven, in his last years, was speaking of experiences which are not normal, but which are nevertheless in the line of human development. But this strange slow movement, as more than one writer has remarked, makes on us the impression of something strictly abnormal. It is as if some racial memory had stirred in him, referring to some forgotten and alien despair. There is here a remote and frozen anguish, wailing over some implacable destiny. This is hardly human suffering; it is more like a memory from some ancient and starless night of the soul. What it is doing in this quartet we cannot imagine. If Beethoven wanted a contrast to the victorious note of the first movement he has certainly got it. But even the magnificent fugue at the end, the most triumphant movement in all Beethoven's quartets, is no resolution of the cold despair of this movement. It does not belong to the same world. Nowhere else has Beethoven's imagination been exercised in so strange a region. The Coriolan overture paints an implacable destiny, and its ending is utter night, yet even here we are dealing with states of the soul that belong to the normal human heritage. The terrible dramas depicted in the first movements of the ninth symphony and the last pianoforte sonata are beyond ordinary human experience but they are, we feel, natural extensions of it.

Each of the three Rasoumovsky quartets has a victorious conclusion, although this conclusion, in the case of the E minor quartet, strikes one as somewhat arbitrary. They are essentially poems of conflict, and although the experiences they communicate are very varied they may be regarded as springing from the root experience that also inspires the C minor symphony. Such a root experience, as we have said before, can assume many different embodiments. A parallel example is probably furnished by Shakespeare's great group of tragedies which, different as they are from one another, surely sprang from some root experience which conditioned his whole attitude towards life.

The first work on a grand scale in which the conflict is taken for granted and ignored, and the fruits of victory enjoyed, is the seventh symphony. In the first movement of this magnificent work we have the impression of a whole world stirring to exultant life. In the year that Beethoven finished the seventh symphony he wrote: "Almighty One, in the woods I am blessed. Happy everyone in the woods. Every tree speaks through thee. O God! What glory in the woodland! On the heights is peace—peace to serve Him." In these stammering words Beethoven expresses something of the joy that is expressed in this symphony. The great introduction to the first movement seems to convey the awakening and murmuring of the multitudinous life of an immense forest. Much more than in the Pastoral symphony do we feel here in the presence of Nature itself.[1] It is life, life in every form, not merely human life, of which the exultation is here expressed. The Allegretto has a similar universal quality. Its dreamy melancholy seems to refer to some universal and far-off sorrow. It passes, like the shadow of a cloud passing across the face of the sun. The exultant note rises higher until, in the last movement, we are in the region of pure ecstasy, a reckless, headlong ecstasy, a more than Bacchic festival of joy. In this symphony Beethoven seems to have emerged into a region where the spiritual struggle that had obsessed him for years is finally done with. Conflict and anguish, to say nothing of despair, are completely absent from this symphony. The hard road to victory, it would appear, has been trodden for the last time. And since this symphony is one of Beethoven's very greatest works we may have confidence that the experience it conveys is fundamental. In the companion symphony, the eighth, the absence of conflict is even more conspicuous. It would seem that Beethoven had won through

[1] I find in the *Revue Musicale* of April 1, 1927, a similar idea expressed by Romain Rolland: speaking of the sixth and seventh symphonies he says: "Dans l'un et l'autre cas, dans les deux Symphonies, une impression dominante de Nature—champs ou forêts, soleil ou nuit—et l'esprit, qui s'assimile à elle, qui épouse ces forces, qui de l'étoffe de ses vibrations, de ses rythmes, de ses lois, de sa substance, tresse un jeu souverain."

to a state of happiness where his great problems were completely solved. And it is probable that if Beethoven had now been able to marry and to enter fully into the warm human world, the music of his last years would have been very different from what it is. What is called his second-period music is essentially concerned, we believe, with the posing and solution of a problem, and it is very probable that at this time Beethoven felt that his problem was solved. The seventh and eighth symphonies were finished in the year 1812, although the sketches for them precede that date by a few years. And at the very time that Beethoven was engaged in giving final artistic expression to the experience that inspires those works he was beginning to realize that the experience was not, for him, a permanent possession.

CHAPTER SIX

Love and Money

FOR NEARLY a decade following the year 1809 Beethoven was singularly unproductive. The general characteristic of his music up to that time is what we may call its victorious quality. The noble spaciousness and confidence of such works as the violin concerto and the Emperor concerto may be found in nearly all the music Beethoven composed from the Eroica symphony to the eighth symphony. It is the work of a man full of confidence, hope, and the consciousness of indomitable power. It had appeared that he was to be shut out from life in its plenitude, that even his passion for creation might be destined to non-fulfilment. But the menace had been faced and had been found to be less terrible than it seemed. His impending deafness, which had bulked so large in Beethoven's imagination, was found to hinder neither his artistic nor, very much, his social activities. During these years it seemed to Beethoven that all things were still possible to him—at a price, it is true, but a price he had found courage enough within himself to pay. The music of this period reflects this consciousness. Again and again, in these compositions, Beethoven's last word is one of exultant confidence. It is significant that not one of Beethoven's compositions after this period culminates in this way. The fugue of the Hammerclavier sonata, and the last movements of the later piano sonatas, the Choral movement of the ninth symphony and the concluding movements of the late quartets, do not repeal this note of personal and unclouded triumph. And, indeed, his triumph was premature. He was to find that the fruits of victory he imagined to be within his grasp were not for him. His courage and resolution, that had taken him so far, were not enough. He had to learn submission and endurance. The key to Beethoven's spiritual development during these musically unproductive years is to be found in the statements in his journal for the years 1812 and 1813.

"Submission, absolute submission to your fate, only this can give you the sacrifice . . . to the servitude—O, hard struggle! Turn everything which remains to be done to planning the long journey—you must yourself find all that your most blessed wish can offer, you must force it to your will—keep always of the same mind.

"*Thou mayest no longer be a man,* not for thyself, only for others, *for thee there is no longer happiness except in thyself, in thy art*—O God, give me strength to conquer myself, nothing must chain me to life. Thus everything connected with A. will go to destruction.

"To forgo a great act which might have been and remain so—O, what a difference compared with

an unstudied life which often arose in my fancy—
O fearful conditions which do not suppress my feeling for domesticity, but whose execution O God,
God look down upon the unhappy B., do not permit
it to last thus much longer—"

These entries are concerned with Beethoven's discovery that he must forgo marriage. The "feeling for
domesticity" to which he refers was very powerful at
this period of Beethoven's life. The "unstudied life" he
pictured must have seemed to him the natural sequel
to what he had achieved. In the year 1810 Beethoven was
forty years of age and, in spite of ill-health, his physical
vitality was such that he appeared no more than thirty.
His fame was great. He was already considered by many
people to be the greatest of all composers. And his financial position had, it appeared, recently been made thoroughly secure. In 1809 he had been invited to Cassel by
the King of Westphalia at a salary of 600 ducats in gold
per annum. He was on the point of accepting this invita-
tion when three aristocrats, the Archduke Rudolf,
Prince Lobkowitz and Prince Kinsky, desiring that he
should remain in Vienna, promised him, between them,
a yearly payment of 4,000 florins. This, combined with
what he could earn by his compositions, would place
him in a sound, though not an affluent, position. These
were the circumstances in which Beethoven contem-
plated marriage. His attitude at this time was a little
curious but not unnatural. It seems to have been the
married state itself that Beethoven craved after rather
than union with some unique and irreplaceable woman.
That he had already had amorous adventures is fairly
clear from certain contemporary references, but he now

wished to "settle down," to have order in his domestic affairs, and to satisfy his craving for companionship. Nevertheless, marriage without love was impossible to Beethoven, and his attitude towards love was essentially romantic. He had, as we have seen, very little understanding of men, and it is probable that he had even less of women. A beautiful face was very likely, for him, to seem the index to a noble mind. In the society in which he had moved feminine elegance and beauty were not rare, and the fact that the women he met were of altogether superior social standing would not greatly affect a man so little diffident as Beethoven. We must picture Beethoven as being, at this time, in a turbulent emotional condition. His creative ability had steadily increased, he had found a way of life in spite of his affliction, and his position was assured. For the first time since he had come to maturity he felt that he could "let himself go" and enter upon his full heritage as a man. A wife, to a man of Beethoven's nature, was absolutely essential to this full human life. The more so, in his case, since his increasing deafness still threatened him at times with a terrible isolation.

These were the circumstances in which Beethoven wrote to Wegeler in Coblenz, on May 2, 1810.

> "A few years ago my quiet, retired mode of life ceased, and I was forcibly drawn into activities of the world; I have not yet formed a favourable opinion of it but rather one against it—but who is there could escape the influence of the external storms? Yet I should be happy, perhaps one of the happiest of men, if the demon had not taken possession of my ears. If I had not read somewhere that

a man may not voluntarily part with his life so long as a good deed remains for him to perform, I should long ago have been no more—and indeed by my own hands. O, life is so beautiful, but to me it is poisoned.

"You will not decline to accede to my friendly request if I beg of you to secure my baptismal certificate for me. Whatever expense may attach to the matter, since you have an account with Steffen Breuning, you can recoup yourself at once from that source, and I will make it good at once to Steffen here. If you should yourself think it worth while to investigate the matter and make the trip from Coblenz to Bonn, charge everything to me. But one thing must be borne in mind, namely, that *there was a brother born before* I was, who was also named Ludwig with the addition Maria, but who died. To fix my age beyond doubt, this brother must first be found, inasmuch as I already know that in this respect mistake has been made by others, and I had been said to be older than I am. Unfortunately I myself lived for a time without knowing my age. I had a family register but it has been lost heaven knows how. Therefore do not be bored if I urge you to attend to this matter, to find Maria and the present Ludwig who was born after him. The sooner you send me the baptismal certificate the greater will be my obligation."

To this we must add three notes to Zmeskall, written in the preceding month.

"Dear Zmeskall, do send me your looking-glass which hangs beside your window for a few hours, mine is broken, if you would be so kind as to buy me one like it to-day it would be a great favour. I'll recoup you for your expenditure at once—forgive my importunity, dear Z."

"Dear Z. do not get angry at my little note—think of the situation which I am in, like Hercules once at Queen Omphale's??? I asked you to buy me a looking-glass like yours, and beg you as soon as you are not using yours which I am returning to send it back to me for mine is broken—farewell and don't again write to me about the great man—for I never felt the strength or weakness of human nature as I feel it just now. Remain fond of me."

"Do not get vexed, dear Z. because of my continued demands upon you—let me know how much you paid for the looking-glass?

"Farewell, we shall see each other soon in the Swan as the food is daily growing worse in the [*illegible*]—I have had another violent attack of colic since day before yesterday, but it is better to-day."

These letters are connected with Beethoven's marriage project of this time; and there is good evidence that he made a formal proposal of marriage to young Therese von Malfatti, daughter of Dr. von Malfatti. She was at this time about nineteen years of age and is reputed to have been one of the most beautiful women in Vienna. Other letters bearing on the matter reveal a curiously painful agitation on Beethoven's part—a sort of self-distrust as of a man attracted against his better judgment. We should probably be right in supposing that Beethoven was, on this occasion, attracted by a beautiful face, a form of attraction which is at once violent and unsatisfactory. However that may be the whole affair fell through very speedily. Beethoven's proposal, if he made one, was refused. The young Bettina Brentano, a friend of Goethe and related to the Brentano family, old friends of Beethoven, came to Vienna just at this time and called on Beethoven. We have already had occasion to point out that the highest value is not to be attributed to this young woman's testimony. Besides her doubtful report of a long conversation with Beethoven, she gives three letters from Beethoven to herself, dated 1810, 1811 and 1812, of which only the second is certainly authentic. The third letter is the most doubtful; it is possible that the first letter was based on actual communications from Beethoven. But for our present purpose the important point that emerges, after allowing everything that can reasonably be urged against Bettina's trustworthiness, is that Beethoven's romantic feelings were once more aroused. There can be little doubt that he talked volubly and excitedly to this sympathetic, clever and highly romantic young girl. It is quite probable that he imagined that he had at last met a real companion. There is no question as to the genuineness of her hero-worship, and she appears to have been prolific in the invention of the sort of vague and high-sounding phrases into which Beethoven could read the deepest wisdom. There is no evidence that he offered marriage to Bettina—probably his very recent experience with the Malfatti was sufficient to deter him—but certainly his "feeling for domesticity" fastened upon her as its next object. It is probable, however, that this feeling did not advance beyond the stage of romantic yearning. In the certainly authentic letter, of February 10, 1811, he says:

"You are to be married, dear Bettina, or have already been, and I could not see you once more before then; may all happiness with which marriage blesses the married, flow upon you. What shall I tell you about myself? 'Pity my fate,' I cry with Johanna; if I can save a few years for myself for that and all other weal and woe I shall thank Him the all-comprehending and Exalted."

At this time, it is evident, whatever hopes Beethoven may have had of Bettina had been abandoned. But there is no evidence that the whole episode was more than a romantic and unserious interlude. It may have distracted Beethoven, but it seems unlikely that it lightened his fundamental depression.

The next episode of this kind occurred in the summer of 1811, when Beethoven was at Teplitz. He there met Amalie Sebald, who had come with Countess von der Recke from Berlin. Amalie is described as having had "a fascinatingly lovely singing voice," and Weber was one of those who conceived a great affection for her. Beethoven appears to have been immediately attracted and that his attentions were not unwelcome is shown by his letter to Tiedge, dated September 6, 1811, sending "to Amalie an ardent kiss when no one sees us." The next year Beethoven visited Teplitz again, and again encountered Amalie Sebald. The following letters are concerned with this period:

"Teplitz, *Sept.* 16, 1812.

"For Amalie von Sebald:

"Tyrant—I? your tyrant? Only a misapprehension can lead you to say this even if your judgment of me indicated no agreement of thought with me! but no blame to you on this account; it is rather a piece of good fortune for you—yesterday I was not wholly well, since this morning I have grown worse; something indigestible was the cause, and the irascible part of me appears to seize upon the bad as well as the good; but do not apply this to my moral nature; people say nothing, they are only people; they generally see only themselves in others, and that is nothing; away with this, the good, the beautiful needs no people. It is here without help and that, after all, appears to be the reason of our agreement. Farewell, dear Amalie; if the moon shines brighter for me this evening than the sun by day you will see with you the least of men."

·

"Dear, good Amalie. After leaving you yesterday, my condition grew worse and from last night till now I have not left my bed, I wanted to send you word yesterday but thought it would look as if I wanted to appear important in your eyes, so I refrained. What dream of yours is this that you are nothing to me, we will talk of that by word of mouth, dear Amalie; I have always wished only that my presence might bring you rest and peace, and that you would have confidence in me; I hope to be better to-morrow and that we may spend the few hours which remain of your sojourn in the enjoyment of nature to our mutual uplift and enlightenment. Good night, dear Amalie, many thanks for your kind thought of your friend."

One more document to this series may be quoted.

(*In Amalie Sebald's handwriting*):

"My tyrant demands an account—here it is:
A fowl 1. fl. U. S.
The soup 9 kr.
"With all my heart I hope that it may agree with you."

(*In Beethoven's handwriting*):

"Tyrants do not pay, but the bill must be receipted, and you can do that best if you come in person. N.B. With the bill to your humbled tyrant."

These letters certainly do not testify to an overwhelming passion on Beethoven's part, but it is possible that the affair was more serious than it seems. The extract we have already quoted from the journal was written at this time, and the concluding sentence, "Thus everything connected with A. will go to destruction," would seem to refer to Amalie. Unfortunately it is not certain that the letter transcribed as an A really is an A. An additional indication that the affair may have been serious is provided by Fanny Giannatasio del Rio's report of a conversation she overheard between Beethoven and her father in September, 1816, when he said that five years before he had got acquainted with a person, union with whom would have been to him the greatest happiness of his life. It was not to be thought of, almost an impossibility, a chimera—nevertheless it is now as on the first day. This harmony, he added, he had not yet discovered. It had never reached a confession, but he could not get it out of his mind.

If the statement "five years before" is to be taken as exact then Amalie Sebald is more closely indicated than any other woman with whom Beethoven had known relations.

However this may be, it is evident that the first years of Beethoven's nonproductive period coincided with a time of restless and unsatisfied yearning for sexual love and for the peace of marriage. It is possible that the famous letter to the "Immortal Beloved," found amongst Beethoven's belongings after his death, belongs to this period, and that it was written to yet another woman. Why, in spite of his desires, Beethoven did not marry at this time, is a matter for conjecture. To women of the kind that attracted him he would hardly have seemed a desirable husband. He was, from their point of view, ugly, poor, ill-bred, and terrifyingly impulsive and self-willed. On the known occasions when he made a proposal of marriage he was refused. And it may be that Beethoven himself came to realize that marriage was impossible for him. It is said that there are indications that he suffered from syphilis, although the precise weight to be given them cannot be decided until the evidence is published. If this be the case then we should require to know at what date Beethoven discovered his condition, and what hopes he may have entertained of a cure. If we make the remark in the journal of 1812, "Thou mayest no longer be a man, not for thyself, only for others," to be an illusion to this disease, we may refer it either to his discovery of his condition or to his realization that it was incurable. In the former case we may suppose that he had hopes of a cure and could still allow himself to yearn after the married state. Yet as long as five or six years later he notes in his journal:

> "Love alone—yes only love can give you a happier life—O God—let me—let me finally find one—who will strengthen me in virtue—who will lawfully be mine."

This remark is very difficult to reconcile with the theory that Beethoven was consciously suffering from a disease that made marriage impossible. At no time of his life is Beethoven's attitude towards marriage easy to reconcile with the syphilis theory, and considering how much of that theory seems to be highly debatable and mere rumour it must at present be ignored. Nevertheless, there are indications that Beethoven, although yearning after the marriage state, felt that it was impossible to him. This realization seems to have been connected, more or less obscurely, with the feeling that his creative activity would be thereby hindered. In a conversation with Schindler in 1823, referring to his rejection of certain advances made recently by the Countess Guicciardi, he said, "And if I had wished to give my vital powers with that life, what would have remained for what is nobler, better?" But even if Beethoven's solitariness was to some extent the result of deliberate sacrifice, it is certain that he felt very hardly the conditions that made that sacrifice necessary. His solitariness was one of the things Beethoven found it hardest to accept. He may have known, with the profound instinctive knowledge of genius, that solitude was necessary to the highest development of his creative power. But to know is not the same thing as to accept, and the full acceptance of his irrevocable and profound loneliness was one of the last and greatest of Beethoven's victories. Already, at the period we are now dealing with, we see on Beethoven's part a consciousness that the attempt to escape his loneliness would be an attempt to cheat his destiny. And his later acceptance of that destiny, although complete, was not incompatible with moods of passionate yearning for what might have been. If, indeed, that destiny was partly due to what Beethoven would consider his own fault we can easily understand that that yearning might rise to an almost intolerable agony. That terrible yearning, a heartache which expresses itself as both a prayer and a sob, is surely the inspiration of one of Beethoven's last and most intimate confessions, the Cavatina of the B flat quartet, of which Beethoven said that never did music of his move him so much. There is here sorrow without hope, sorrow for what is irrevocable, and a longing for what has not been and never can be. But although Beethoven could experience such moods up to the very end, how far he had advanced is shown by the movement that originally followed this, the *Grosse Fuge*. An indomitable will is here expressed that is both creative and submissive; the conditions of creation have been accepted by a one-time uncontrollable creative energy. We have here the achievement that follows on sacrifice, and in face of this achievement the Cavatina remains in our memory merely as a record of the price that has been well paid. More than anything else in music this *Grosse Fuge*, regarded as the crown of the whole wonderful quartet, justifies the ways of God to men.

We have already mentioned that, in 1809, arrangements were made that seemed to make Beethoven's financial position assured. No man, more than the serious artist, craves an independent income. To no other class of man is the freedom it assures so valuable. The feeling that one is working under pressure, that one is not free to develop, revise and extend, that one has no time to explore one's deepest depths, is intolerable except to those whose fluency is only another aspect of their superficiality. To Beethoven, who of all artists had the greatest depths to explore, the terrible urge of mere poverty was particularly hateful and, as we shall see later, he would take any steps possible to circumvent it. His exultation, therefore, when the three Princes contacted to give him an annuity was great and justifiable. But his hopes proved to be unfounded. His annuity contract bore the date March 1, 1809, but on March 15, 1811, the Austrian *Finanz-Patent* came into force, whereby bank-notes were reduced to one-fifth of their value. The Princes should, in equity, have made the difference up to Beethoven, and the Archduke Rudolf did so. The others, however, did not give Beethoven the same security. Beethoven's income was very greatly reduced, for the Archduke's contribution to the total 4,000 florins was little more than one-third. But Beethoven was to be even worse off than this would indicate. In November, 1812, Prince Kinsky, whose promised contribution had been the largest of the three, was thrown from his horse and killed. As a result, nothing was paid to Beethoven from Kinsky's estate from November 3, 1812, to March 31, 1815. Before this the other guarantor, Prince Lobkowitz, had gone bankrupt, and

Beethoven received nothing from him from September 1, 1811, to April 19, 1815. Beethoven's cherished dream of independence, therefore, was dissipated almost as soon as it arose. This experience had a powerful effect on Beethoven. We must remember that he lived in a period of war and great uncertainty. His experience with his three Princes brought the uncertainty of human affairs home to him more forcibly than ever. We must remember also that his contempt for most of his fellow-men was strong and genuine. From his point of view an astonishingly large proportion of his associates were scoundrels. Apart from their observance of the law the only possible ideals they had, to Beethoven's perception, were enshrined in that curious code of ethics called "business morality," a code for which Beethoven did not feel any overwhelming and innate reverence. Of publishers, in particular, in whose persons he had most closely observed the workings of business morality, he had the lowest opinion. He expressly refused to make any distinction between them. To Beethoven, at this time, therefore, came the realization that he must fight for his own land. He lived in a world that he despised, and he felt that it must be fought with its own weapons. The practical consequences of this realization become most prominent in his negotiations for the sale of the great Mass in D, which we shall discuss later. At the moment it is sufficient to notice that Beethoven's estimate of his own character and of that of the world at large was perfectly sincere. His reactions to everything were violent and direct. He lacked tolerance just as he lacked cynicism. His judgments, even when they agreed with conventional judgments, were not adopted from conventionality. No man was ever more completely loyal to his own experience than was Beethoven. And it is a corollary that no man was ever less ashamed of himself than was Beethoven. A failure to understand these characteristics of Beethoven's leads to ludicrously incoherent views of his psychology. Thus Mr. Krehbiel, in his edition of Thayer's *Life of Beethoven*, states:

> "Careful readers of this biography can easily recall a number of lapses from high ideals of candour and justice in his treatment of his friends and of a nice sense of honour and honesty in his dealings with his publishers; but at no time have these blemishes been so numerous or so patent as they are in the negotiations for the publication of the *Missa Solemnis*—a circumstance which is thrown into a particularly strong light by the frequency and vehemence of his protestations of moral rectitude in the letters which have risen like ghosts to accuse him, and by the strange paradox that the period is one in which his artistic thoughts and imagination dwelt in the highest regions to which they ever soared."

The "paradox" exists only if it be supposed that Beethoven's "lapses" were recognized by himself as such. All that we know of the man is against such a supposition. His morality, as is the case with most artists, was not identical with that professed by business men. His morality may perhaps be summed up as consisting of unfaltering courage in being true to his own experience. The *Missa Solemnis* would indeed be a marvel if produced by a conscious hypocrite, and so would almost everything else that Beethoven wrote. That note of authenticity that we find in all Beethoven's greatest music is incompatible with anything less than complete sincerity on the part of the man. Beethoven really felt what he professed to feel. His music is incompatible with any other assumption; it is not in the least incompatible with artfulness and unscrupulousness in dealing with publishers. That a man should write the *Missa Solemnis* and at the same time fail to fulfil certain commercial contracts may or may not be an interesting psychological fact. It only becomes a moral problem and the *Missa Solemnis* a paradox if it be assumed that the creation of the *Missa Solemnis* implies a reverence for contracts. That it implies a mighty courage, an indomitable spirit, a profound emotional experience, together with an immense power of co-ordinating them and a prodigious genius in expressing them, is obvious. Only a very great spirit could have written the *Missa Solemnis*. And it is highly probable that a man guilty of certain moral "lapses" could not attain such heights. But that a certain unscrupulousness in relation to publishers is not incompatible with such heights is proved by the existence of the *Missa Solemnis*. It is obvious that whatever moral canons Beethoven violated he did not violate his own, and that they were of a sufficiently lofty character to give us the music we have. We may wish that to his other virtues he had added "a nice sense of honour and honesty in his dealings with his publishers," but it seems evident that the virtues he had were even more rare and more valuable, and the fact that they did not imply that "niceness" is merely a not very interesting fact about what we may call the natural history of genius.

We have seen that the early part of Beethoven's unproductive years coincided with the failure of his marriage projects and with the disappointment of his hopes of a settled income. To these we must add sickness, and anxiety caused by his brothers. His brother Johann had formed an irregular union with a Therese Obermayer and it appears to have come to Beethoven's ears that he was about to marry the girl. Beethoven's moral code seems always to have been particularly hard on women of loose character, and he evidently felt very strongly on the prospect of having such a one as a relative. He therefore journeyed to Linz in order to stop the marriage, if possible. The measures he took to accomplish his end were violent and tactless. He pushed them so far as to obtain a police order that the girl should be removed to Vienna if, on a certain day, she should still be found in Linz. But Beethoven's one way of overcoming opposition, by force and still more force, was this time ineffective. Johann countered by marrying the girl. Thus Beethoven had brought about the very result he feared. This episode is a good illustration of Beethoven's extraordinary lack of understanding of normal people. In trying to override his brother as he did he was treating him with the same contempt he had for most men, but this time it was violent and passionate. There is evidence, also, that he had of this brother a specially low opinion.

At about this time Beethoven's other brother, Carl, was taken ill, and Beethoven, out of his small resources, had to come to his assistance. Beethoven writes that he had wholly to support "an unfortunate sick brother together with his family," and it is certain that he had very largely to supply them even with the necessaries of life. A glimpse of Beethoven's own position at this time is given us in Spohr's *Autobiography*, where he says:

> "He was not a good housekeeper and had the ill-luck to be robbed by those about him. So he often lacked necessities. In the early part of our acquaintance I once asked him, after he had been absent from the eating-house: 'You were not ill, were you?'—'My boots were, and as I have only one pair I had house-arrest,' was the answer. Frau Streicher, also, 'found Beethoven in the summer of 1813, in the most desolate state as regards his physical and domestic needs—not only did he not have a single good coat, but not a whole shirt.'"

Beethoven's state at this time was partly due to his natural carelessness about money, for he had until a few years before been receiving fair sums from his publishers. From this time on he became more careful with money when he got it and, as we have said, he made more strenuous efforts to get it. The following two letters to Varena, who had previously got him to lend his services in aid of a charity concert, throw light upon his general attitude at this time.

> "Dear Sir!
>
> "No doubt Rode was right in all he said about me; my health is not of the best and without fault of my own my condition otherwise is perhaps more unfavourable than at any time in my life; but neither this nor anything else shall dissuade me from helping the equally innocent sufferers, the convent ladies, so far as my mortal talents will permit. To this end, two entirely new symphonies

are at your services, an air for bass voice with chorus, several smaller single choruses—if you need the overture to Hungary's Benefactor which you performed last year, it is at your service.

"The Overture to 'The Ruins of Athens,' although in a smaller style, is also at your service. Amongst the choruses is a chorus of Dervishes, a good signboard for a mixed public.

"In my opinion you would do best to choose a day on which you could give the oratorio 'Christus am Olberg'; since then it has been played all over; this would then fill half the concert; for the second half you would play a new symphony, the overture and different choruses, as also the bass air with chorus mentioned; thus the evening would not be without variety; but you would better talk this over with the musical councillors in your city and let them decide. What you say concerning remuneration for me from a third person I think I can guess who he is; if I were in my former condition I would flatly say: 'Beethoven never takes pay when the benefiting of humanity is concerned,' but now, placed in a condition through my great benevolence (the cause of which can bring me no shame) and other circumstances which are to blame, which are caused by men without honesty or honour, I say frankly I would not decline such an offer from a rich third party; but there is no thought of a demand; even if there should prove to be nothing in the talk about a third person, be convinced that I am just as willing now to be of service to my friends, the reverend women, as I was last year without the least reward, and as I shall always be to suffering humanity as long as I breathe. And now farewell. Write to me soon and I will care for all that is necessary with the greatest zeal.

"My best wishes for the convent."

On April 8, 1813, he writes again:

"My dear V!

"I received with much pleasure your letter but again with much displeasure the 100 florins sent by the poor cloister ladies; meanwhile they are deposited with me to be applied to the payment of the expenses for copying. Whatever remains will be returned to the noble cloister women together with a view of the accounts.

"For such occasions I never accept anything—I thought that the third person to whom you referred was perhaps the ex-King of Holland and—yes, from him who probably took from the Hollanders in a less righteous way I would have no hesitation in accepting something in my present condition; now, however, I beg kindly that nothing more be said on the subject. Write me your opinion as to whether if I came to Gratz I could give a concert; for it is not likely that Vienna will long remain my place of residence; perhaps it is already too late, but your opinion on the subject will always be welcome.

"The works will be copied and as soon as possible you shall have them—do whatever you please with the oratorio; whenever it can do any good my purposes will best be subserved.

"All things beautiful to our Ursulines, whom I am glad to be able to serve again."

Beethoven's reference to Louis Bonaparte, the ex-King of Holland "who probably took from the Hollanders in a less righteous way," is an interesting indication of his moral attitude where money was concerned. It appears that he regarded any well-off person that he considered a swindler as fair game. The "men without honesty or honour" is doubtless a reference to the Princes whose contributions had ceased. Another illustration of Beethoven's moral code, although not of the clearest, is provided by his treatment of Maezel over the "Battle symphony." This work, the worst that Beethoven ever wrote, and the only one that achieved great popularity in his lifetime, was originally suggested by the showman Maezel to be composed for his machine, the Panharmonicon. It was decided, however, to compose it for orchestra. Beethoven treated the whole thing as a joke, as did the eminent musicians who gave their services for the performance. It turned out, however, to be a highly profitable joke, and when Maezel claimed the score, on the ground that it had been composed for his instrument, Beethoven refused to give it to him. Maezel had gone to considerable trouble and expense on account of this work and felt that he had a right to it. He therefore stole the parts and left Vienna with them. Beethoven, so far from feeling guilty in the matter, was highly indignant and immediately instituted proceedings against Maezel. The affair dragged on for some years, but was finally settled amicably. The episode is interesting as helping to confirm our contention that Beethoven did not regard his financial transactions as immoral. Nobody can study the part Beethoven played in this affair without realizing that he felt himself to be thoroughly in the right.

A number of biographers, following Thayer, have deplored Beethoven's conduct in this and other business transactions. That conduct, when examined, appears by no means scurrilous enough to warrant so much pious horror, but apart from the exaggeration the attitude is harmful for directing attention to the wrong thing. Beethoven's morality was of the noblest, although it was not indentical with business morality. The ideal business man is doubtless a very high order of being, but Beethoven's spiritual excellence was of another kind. It is surely somewhat gratuitous to suppose that the extent to which a man falls short of business morality is a measure of the extent to which he is inferior as a spiritual being. Those who have any conception of the moral qualities required to be as utterly faithful to his experience and genius as was Beethoven will not deny him his place in the constellation of the virtuous, although his light is perhaps more fitful and certainly more fiery than the calm radiance of the perfect business man. But Thayer is so horrified at Beethoven's quiet limited unscrupulousness where publishers were concerned that he finds faults where there are none and misses magnificent virtues on the same page. Thus he blames Beethoven, who had sold four compositions to Mr. Birchall for sixty-five pounds, for asking for another fifty shillings to cover copying and postage expenses. It is very obvious that Beethoven felt within his rights in asking for this money, and it seems very clear that he was. Thayer is apparently shocked to find that Beethoven, having received sixty-five pounds, did not pay the other expenses himself. He seems to think that it indicates an undesirable money-grubbing spirit. Yet at this same time, the year 1816, Beethoven refused an offer from General Kyd to compose a symphony for one hundred pounds, with a good prospect of making one thousand pounds by profits on performances by the London Philharmonic Society, and he refused this commission solely because the General wanted the symphony to be written in his earlier manner. Further, he refused unhesitatingly and violently. Here Beethoven's own, true moral code was involved and his desire for money had no chance against it. When Dr. Bertolini, a perfectly honourable man in business matters, but unacquainted with Beethoven's code of morals, congratulated him on what he thought an unexceptionable offer he was surprised when Beethoven "declared that he would receive dictation from no one; he needed no money, despised it and would not submit himself to the whim of another man for half the world, still less compose anything which was not according to his liking, to his individuality. From that time he was also cool towards Bertolini and remained so." And probably Bertolini never understood that his offence, on the Beethoven code of ethics, was his assumption that Beethoven would act as a scoundrel. Simrock, in his account of the incident, says that "In his excitement he expressed himself very angrily and with deep displeasure towards a nation which by such an offer had manifested so low an opinion of an artist and art, which he looked upon as a great insult." This incident should have suggested to Thayer and to the biographers who follow him that we are here in the presence of two moral codes, and that to Beethoven the excellent General Kyd was doubtless an abandoned and worthless scoundrel. And it is not clear that Beethoven's code is inferior to that of business morality if we are to adopt the criterion that it is by their fruits we shall know them.

CHAPTER SEVEN

The Hammerclavier Sonata

BEETHOVEN's non-productivity during the years 1810–17 was only partly due to "external storms." His non-productivity was not absolute, but none of his greatest works were originated and matured during this period. Such works, in the case of Beethoven, always sprang from some profound and mastered experience. The same root experience could serve as the spiritual content of many different works, for any such experience is rich in aspects and may be explored from many points of view. Thus both the Eroica and C minor symphonies are inspired by the same root experience, but they are entirely distinct works of art. Such an experience is really composed of many elements which can be formed by the artist into different organic wholes. So far as the inner history of Beethoven's non-productive years are concerned we may regard them as occupied by the assimilation of another root experience, an experience which, by the nature of the case, could only gradually be realized. This experience was his growing consciousness that what is called the "human" life, the life that includes love, marriage, children, friends, was withheld from him. This emotional and passionate man was condemned to a fundamental isolation from the warm human community. How much this isolation meant to Beethoven we see most clearly in his behaviour in connection with his nephew Carl. Into this one narrow channel was poured Beethoven's wealth of emotion; from this one being he demanded the love and sympathy that had been denied him; and the young man very nearly died under the strain. But Beethoven's idolatrous love for his nephew was merely a blind, irrational, pitiful attempt to make at least one point of contact with that warm human world from which he was shut out. Deep within himself the artist in him knew that his isolation was irretrievable. Personal relations, that should give him a sense of completeness and satisfy his hunger, were impossible. Henceforth his only escape from an isolation become intolerable was to reach out to an Eternal Father, to God the Companion, or to merge his private aspirations into the aspirations of mankind at large.

At the time that he wrote the Hammerclavier sonata, finished in 1818, Beethoven's realization of his essential loneliness was terrible and complete. But we may suppose that even then he was becoming aware that his separation from the world was the entry into a different and more exalted region. But the Hammerclavier sonata is the expression of a man of infinite suffering, of infinite courage and will, but without God and without hope. At the time that he depicted this experience it is possible that Beethoven had already passed beyond it. The sonata is the complete expression of an important stage in Beethoven's spiritual development, but it was only after passing through this stage that the wonderful new world lay open before him, and that all his greatest work was achieved. From the Hammerclavier sonata itself nothing more could come. Its spiritual content is at the end of a process, an end that contains within itself no new beginning. The completely naked Beethoven, relying upon nothing whatever but his inner resources, has said his last word in the Hammerclavier sonata. Without some new life added to him, without some new organization of his experience, the undying energy of the Hammerclavier fugue can be used only to say over again what it has already said. The Hammerclavier sonata does not, in its spiritual content, belong to what is called Beethoven's third period. Neither does it belong to his second. It stands alone, a great and grim memorial to the long and painful journey between the two worlds.

The courage and resolution we find in the first movement is curiously austere. The old experience is once again to be lived through, but the spirit in which it is approached is very different. Those cold harmonies, so characteristic of Beethoven's later work, no longer convey the warm human confidence of a man who knows that victory lies at the end. There is expressed a stark, bare resolution, courageous enough, but uncoloured by any joy in conflict. And the other elements that go to make up the wealth of a Beethoven first movement have all become colder. The man who wrote this music is already a great solitary. He has abated nothing of his courage, but it has become more grim. Suffering, it would appear, has hardened him; never again, one would think, can this man melt. And there is no good-humour in the Scherzo. A curiously laconic savagery, with hints of the formidable passion that is expressing itself so abruptly, entirely separate this movement from the frank energy of the earlier Scherzos. The slow movement is the deliberate expression, by a man who knows no reserves, of the cold and immeasurable woe in whose depths, it would seem, nothing that we could call life could endure. It seems as inimical to human existence as the icy heart of some remote mountain lake. Whether it be faithfulness to psychological experience, or whether it be the instinct of an unmatched artist, the Largo that follows the slow movement is a miracle of art. To end with the slow movement would be unendurable, and any sudden shattering of the hypnotic state it produces would be equally unendurable. The gradual awakening effected by the Largo from our state of dumb suspension fulfils a craving of the spirit that surely only this one artist could ever have formulated. And we awake to what? To the blind and desperate energy left in this man when there was no longer any reason to live. We are presented here with a will to live which is inexpressibly furious and inexpressibly bare. It is the expression of the final refusal of annihilation, even if no hope and no object be left in life. The sheer blind energy, this insistence on mere existence, does not contain within itself dramatic contrasts. To be expressed at all it must be expressed in a form within which its swiftness and violence can rage unchecked. No form permits so unidirectional and un-hampered a flow as the fugue, and Beethoven chose the fugue. And having chosen it, he exhausts its resources to keep his mass moving with the requisite momentum. At one point the mass rises to a climax and there is an interruption. We are given a glimpse, a few bars, dolce and cantabile, of that serene, inhuman eternity that surrounds this blind, furious striving. But it is only a glimpse, a meaningless stare, and we are once more involved in this headlong rush, this most primitive, fundamental and unconquerable of the impulses that manifest themselves in creatures that have life. The spiritual content of this fugue is the fitting complement to the Adagio, in the sense that nothing else could have survived. And the greatness of Beethoven is shown in the fact that having passed through an experience that left him so little to express he yet expressed so much.

CHAPTER EIGHT

God the Companion

OF BEETHOVEN'S religious beliefs we know very little except that they were not orthodox. That Beethoven, towards the end, came to possess a mystical apprehension of life is indisputable, but it is probable that this mystical outlook would have been, in his case, more recalcitrant even than usual to exposition in words. But, so far as these things may be expressed in words, we may conclude, from his own remarks, that he believed in an ultimate, benign and intelligent Power, and that he believed that existence was planned and purposeful. Such beliefs, so expressed, are mere shells that can contain a great variety of contents. Beethoven's Mass in D shows that some of his most important experiences could be contained within the shell of words provided by the mass. But it would be unsafe to conclude from this, as some writers have done, that the usual interpretation of the words of the mass was Beethoven's interpretation. The impression that the music of the Mass makes, in fact, is, that it is a curious blend of the personal and the dramatic or, as we may say, of the subjective and the objective. The Credo of the Mass in D has an overwhelming note of authenticity; the words doubtless expressed something of which Beethoven was passionately convinced; but his conviction was probably better expressed in the mystical sentences he was fond of copying down from Eastern literature. Such phrases as "I am that which is. I am all that was, that is, and that shall be," part of a creed that Beethoven copied out in his own handwriting and kept permanently framed on his desk, probably expressed better, through their very vagueness, Beethoven's intuitions. The very definiteness of the words of the mass, by going beyond Beethoven's personal experience, caused him to treat them, at times, dramatically. The words became, at times, a libretto. But the libretto could, at nearly all points, be made to correspond more or less adequately to a personal experience. The fact that the correspondence is not at all points complete accounts for the curious mixed effect the music makes on us, so that it appears both personal and dramatic. Those who find in the words of the mass an entirely adequate expression of their beliefs are probably justified, therefore, in finding Beethoven's treatment of them too "poetical."

In the Choral movement of the ninth symphony Beethoven is in less exalted regions. Here he finds a solution of his intolerable yearning by making himself one with the whole human family, considered as the children of a Heavenly Father. The solution is a natural one, and is apparently as "lofty" as could be desired, but it is nevertheless felt as an inadequate culmination of the spiritual process portrayed in the first three movements. It is usual to attribute this inadequacy to the employment of the human voice. It is doubtful, however, whether this is the real reason. It is rather that we feel that the spirit which has climbed up the heights of those three movements should now, like Moses on Sinai, be granted a vision of God Himself. To turn back from the serene, unearthly heights of that great Adagio to the warm human world of humanitarian ideals and optimistic rejoicings, is to disappoint our expectation of, and craving for, some ultimate sublimity. That the human voice alone is not responsible is obvious from the Mass. The cause lies deeper, in the very character of the music. The aspiration expressed in the Choral movement, lofty as it is, is not an adequate culmination of the experiences described in the first three movements. That Beethoven himself felt this inadequacy is nearly certain from the evidence we have, and also from the fact that he had the greatest difficulty in making a plausible bridge passage to the last movement from the other three. This movement may be taken, indeed, as the one instance of his failure, in a major work, to rise to the height of his great argument. And the argument was the greatest that he had yet presented. To compare the ninth symphony with the fifth is to realize how greatly this man had grown in spiritual stature. That early, almost boyish idea of fate has become a much profounder conception in this first movement. Fate is no longer personified as some sort of powerful enemy that sufficient courage can defy, even if hopelessly. It is now a truly universal destiny, too complete to evoke any thought of resistance. The brooding mystery from which the theme emerges is, like the primeval darkness that preceded creation, something that conditions the human world, but which is not part of it. And this extra-human power, as presented to us here, has nothing benevolent about it, necessary as it may be for the moulding of the human soul. As the answer to this fate theme Beethoven gives us no more than submission and resignation. But even resignation is overborne and crushed by this implacable destiny, and towards the end of this terrible movement, in the passage for strings that begins on the 513th bar, we are left with nothing but utter despair and pain through which the great fate theme sweeps to its final assertion. After this experience we know, with Beethoven, exactly what to expect, and in the Scherzo we have once more that unconquerable uprising of blind energy that was the very core of the man. This Scherzo is as headlong a movement as the fugue of the Hammerclavier sonata, but there is a fierce joyousness in it quite absent from that work. It is, indeed, part of an organic structure that reaches out to a quite different culmination, although that culmination is not the personal victory of the early works. The Adagio alone would, one thinks, be a sufficiently great culmination. That state of what we can only call serenity based, not on any turning away from suffering, but on its acceptance, is sufficient justification, surely, for the experience portrayed in the first movement. So great a degree of understanding, in which nothing is ignored, is worth, it would seem, whatever price has been paid for it. But there is a state beyond, a condition of almost superhuman ecstasy, as Beethoven had already revealed to us in the last movement of the last pianoforte sonata. The

Adagio of the ninth symphony remains purely human and personal and Beethoven was, at this time, reaching out after something that should transcend what is called the human. He was, at this time, exploring a new region of consciousness. In the late pianoforte sonatas we get more than glimpses of a new state of being as revealed in a music utterly unlike any other music. In the late quartets he was to reveal to us even more unambiguously this new region. In the ninth symphony, however, he could not, for some reason, order this new experience on the scale required. It may be that Beethoven was moving about in worlds not realized. He had, in the late pianoforte sonatas and in the Mass, given us glimpses of this new kind of awareness. He had probably said all that he could, at the moment, say. So he turned from his personal and solitary adventure as a forerunner of the human race to be a partaker in the joy and aspirations of his fellows. This is the last occasion on which Beethoven addresses his fellow-men as one of them. Henceforth he voyaged "in strange seas of thought, alone."

While working on the Mass Beethoven was much troubled with lawsuits relating to his nephew Carl. His brother Carl had, on his death, left his son to the joint guardianship of his wife and of Beethoven. The wife was undoubtedly a woman of loose character, and Beethoven was firmly convinced that she was a merely evil and corrupting influence. He spent a great deal of time and trouble in endeavouring to separate the son entirely from her, an attempt in which he never wholly succeeded. His own love for the nephew was idolatrous, and in opposing the mother he showed quite extraordinary passion and determination. This was partly due to certain notions of duty that he took very seriously but it was, in the main, the outcome of his long repressed craving, now become almost irresistible, for love and intimacy with at least one human being. Carl appears to have been a perfectly average young man, fond of billiards and associating a good deal with prostitutes. Beethoven, putting a good deal down to the account of the mother, seems to have regarded him as a brand to be plucked from the burning. His way of achieving this end, which was to alternate extravagant affection with morose suspicion, led the young man to attempt suicide. Beethoven's relations with his nephew caused him, almost continually, great anxiety. On one occasion, owing to a trifling escapade of his nephew's, he was almost out of his mind for a few days. In addition he was, during this period, continually poor (for he made it a point of honour not to touch the invested money destined for his nephew), his health was bad, and his domestic affairs were atrocious. Although he was now at the very height of his creative power, producing his greatest music, he worked very slowly. What he now had to express was much more difficult to formulate than anything he had previously expressed. The states of consciousness with which he was concerned contained more and more elusive elements, and came from greater depths. The task of creation necessitated an unequalled degree of absorption and withdrawal. The regions within which Beethoven the composer now worked were, to an unprecedented degree, withdrawn and sheltered from his outward life. His deafness and solitariness are almost symbolic of his complete retreat into his inner self. No "external storms" could now influence his work; at most they could interrupt it. The music of the last quartets comes from the profoundest depths of the human soul that any artist has ever sounded.

CHAPTER NINE

The Last Quartets

BEETHOVEN was already thinking of writing a string quartet, a form he had neglected for thirteen years, when a letter came from Prince Galitzin requesting that he should compose three quartets at fifty ducats apiece. Beethoven accepted this offer in January, 1823, but the first quartet, in E flat major, Op. 127, was not finished until early in 1825. It was first performed on March 6, 1825. Two more quartets followed and were sent to the Prince. The Prince had paid for the first quartet, but he never paid Beethoven for the others. It was not until some years after the composer's death, as the result of very strong representations made to him, that the Prince paid over the rest of the money to Beethoven's nephew Carl. But, in writing the three quartets, Beethoven had by no means exhausted the ideas he could embody in this form, and he went on and completed two others, one in C sharp minor, Op. 131, and the other in F major, Op. 135. In these five quartets we have the greatest of Beethoven's music, and much of it is different in kind from any other music that he or anybody else ever wrote. In the last quartets, and particularly in the great three, those in A minor, B flat major, and C sharp minor, Beethoven is exploring new regions of consciousness. All the major, formative experiences of his life had been assimilated; life had nothing new to teach him. And his experience had, as we have seen, taken on a very high degree of organization, and to these organic wholes, formed very deep down in his consciousness, he had given expression again and again. But this inner world to which Beethoven had now retreated, although it no longer owed anything to fresh contacts with the outer world, was nevertheless a living and developing world. It not only contained elements which he had never before explored, but also elements that had never before existed. The last quartets testify to a veritable growth of consciousness, to a higher degree of consciousness, probably, than is manifested anywhere else in art. The human consciousness is a developing thing. It is nourished and fructified by experience but there must be, in addition, an inner principle of growth. A marked increase of consciousness, so far as the human race as a whole is concerned, seems to take æons to manifest itself. But great artists appear who possess a higher degree of consciousness than that enjoyed by the ordinary man. And amongst such artists are some whose growth in awareness, in sensibility, in power of co-ordination, is apparent during their lifetime. In Beethoven such a process is very marked, more marked, probably, than in the case of any other artist. His quite exceptional characteristics and circumstances are partly responsible for this, and may serve to explain his uniqueness. His faithfulness to his experience, his lack of malleability, his deafness, and his emotional isolation from the world, were all favouring conditions for the development of his inner life. This development, as we have said, is very marked from the fifth to the ninth symphonies, for example. The ninth symphony shows a way of apprehending reality, due to the emergence in Beethoven of a new kind of awareness, that was strictly impossible to the young Beethoven. It is a revelation of existence as seen from the vantage point of a higher consciousness. In the ninth symphony Beethoven has, in this respect, so far surpassed the norm of great artists that he cannot influence them. The human mind may be likened to some kind of multiple plant, here in full bloom, there still in the bud. Different minds have flowered in different ways. Beethoven had reached relative maturity in directions where those of us who respond to him are still in the stage of embryonic growth. And in some people, it is obvious, there is no germ of consciousness akin to the state of awareness manifested by the late Beethoven. In his earlier works, however, he is concerned with states of consciousness that most of us can share. For this reason his earlier work has influenced other musicians, in content as well as in form. But there is no music subsequent to Beethoven whose spiritual content is of the order expressed in the ninth symphony. No other musician has ever risen to the state of awareness necessary to write the first movement of that symphony, or possessed the power of synthesizing his experience necessary to write its third movement. Beethoven has shown that it is within the resources of music to express these states of consciousness but, of the great followers of Beethoven, neither Wagner nor Brahms has been in a position to profit by the demonstration. When we come to the last quartets we find a still more remote spiritual content. We here become aware not only of new syntheses of spiritual elements, but of radically new elements. In these "strange seas of thought" Beethoven has discovered unsuspected islands and even continents.

The actual process of what we have called a growth of consciousness is extremely obscure. When we speak of a new synthesis of spiritual elements, whether these elements be emotions or states of awareness or whatever we choose to call them, we must remember that the synthesis corresponds to a definitely new state of consciousness and is not to be described by tabulating its elements. Thus the complex emotion, awe, to a person who has never felt it, does not become known through a knowledge of its constituents. Language, as we have had occasion to remark before, is poor in names for subjective states, and this poverty becomes particularly apparent when we try to describe such works of art as the late quartets. A spiritual synthesis, when we try to describe it, sometimes seems to contain contradictory elements. Thus a conscientious logician would probably hesitate to describe some emotional state as "gay melancholy." Yet, as a blunt description of the *alla tedesca* movement of the B flat quartet, it might pass. Neither word by itself would be in the least adequate. Both elements are present, not as contrasting, but strangely unified in one haunting phrase. And it would not be sufficient to say of the phrase that it is unique. All musical phrases are unique. Merely to say that the phrase is unique ignores the fact that it does suggest certain states rather than others. "Gay melancholy" may be contradictory and is certainly inadequate. But it is no more contradictory and is certainly less inadequate than "tender rage," or "virile weakness" or many other combinations would be.

The musical phrase we have referred to presents, in a simple form, one of the difficulties that faces the writer who wishes to deal with the last string quartets. It is a difficulty which, to a greater or less extent, is involved in any description of a musical composition. But in the last string quartets spiritual experiences are communicated of which it is very difficult to mention even the elements. And yet it is just this music that most moves us and impresses us as containing the profoundest and most valuable experiences that any artist has yet conveyed. Our experience of the opening fugue of the C sharp minor quartet, for example, is surely one of the most pregnant and exalted that we know. Yet Wagner described this movement as the greatest expression of melancholy in all music. One may understand him saying this, and yet be utterly unable to agree with him. It is possible he did not agree with himself. That he heard more than melancholy in this movement we may be convinced, but for the something more he had no words. And yet the presence of that something more makes his description not only inadequate, but entirely erroneous. What is communicated to us in the first movement of the C sharp minor quartet has no more to do with melancholy than it has with joy. All art exists to communicate states of consciousness which are higher synthetic wholes than those of ordinary experience, but in these last quartets Beethoven is dealing with states for which there are no analogues in any other art. Regarding the content of some of his earlier work he could refer a questioner to Shakespeare. Regarding the content of these works he could refer him to nobody.

The first of the last quartets, in E flat major, stands rather apart from the next three, as does the last, in F major, Op. 135. The middle three quartets were worked upon almost simultaneously, they contain some of the same thematic material, they are sufficiently akin for movements originally destined for one to be transferred to another, and in each of them Beethoven abandons the four-movement sonata form. The first of these three quartets, in A minor, Op. 132, has five movements; the second, in B flat major, Op. 130, has six movements; and the third, in C sharp minor, Op. 131, has seven movements. Both Op. 127 and Op. 135 have the usual four-movement form. The middle three quartets are the greatest of the five and it is here that Beethoven the explorer is most clearly revealed. The reason why these quartets, particularly those in B flat major and C sharp minor, are not in sonata form, is made evident by their contents. The four-movement sonata form corresponds to a very fundamental and general psychological process, which is the reason why it is found so satisfactory and has been so often employed. The general scheme of a first movement, usually representing a conflict of some kind, followed by a meditative or consoling slow movement, and that by a section easing the way to a vigorous final statement, to the conclusion won, is, in its main lines, admirably adapted to exhibit an important and recurrent psychological process. The life-histories of many major psychological processes can be accommodated within this framework. But in the quartets we are discussing Beethoven's experience could not be presented in this form. The connection between the various movements is altogether more organic than that of the four-movement sonata form. In these quartets the movements radiate, as it were, from a central experience. They do not represent stages in a journey, each stage being independent and existing in its own right. They represent separate experiences, but the meaning they take on in the quartet is derived from their relation to a dominating, central experience. This is characteristic of the mystic vision, to which everything in the world appears unified in the light of one fundamental experience. In these quartets, then, Beethoven is not describing to us a spiritual history; he is presenting to us a vision of life. In each quartet many elements are surveyed, but from one central point of view. They are presented as apprehended by a special kind of awareness, they are seen in the light of one fundamental experience. It is not any kinship between the experiences described in the separate movements themselves, but the light in which they are seen, that gives to these works their profound homogeneity. Without this unity the quartets could only appear incoherent and capricious. And yet, although the unity possessed by these quartets is of this subtle kind, it is remarkable how generally it has been perceived. Although these quartets do not obey the usual criteria of coherence, they have been felt by nearly all musicians to be quite exceptionally organic. In both the B flat major and C sharp minor quartets Beethoven has given us, quite nakedly, the vision or experience from which the whole work proceeds. In the C sharp minor quartet this dominating experience is found in the fugue with which the work opens. In the B flat quartet it is found in the original last movement, the *Grosse Fuge,* now published separately as Op. 133.

The difference between these two quartets is profound. In the great fugue of the B flat quartet the experiences of life are seen as the conditions of creation and are accepted as such. The fugue has been called an expression of the reconciliation of freedom and necessity, or of assertion and submission, and the terms may pass since they suggest the state of consciousness that informs the fugue, a state in which the apparently opposing elements of life are seen as necessary and no longer in opposition. Beethoven had come to realize that his creative energy, which he at one time opposed to his destiny, in reality owed its very life to that destiny. It is not merely that he believed that the price was worth paying; he came to see it as necessary that a price should be paid. To be willing to suffer in order to create is one thing; to realize that one's creation necessitates one's suffering, that suffering is one of the greatest of God's gifts, is almost to reach a mystical solution of the problem of evil, a solution that it is probably for the good of the world that very few people will ever entertain. Yet, except in terms of this kind, we cannot represent to ourselves the spiritual content of the *Grosse Fuge.* The fugue opens with such an expression of unbridled energy and dominant will that it seems about to break the bounds of the string quartet. This vigorous, striving life is very different from the almost subhuman furious activity of the fugue of the Hammerclavier sonata, although it seems to promise an equally headlong course. But, with the entry of the opposing G flat major episode it changes its character. We become aware that a truly indescribable synthesis has been effected. There is no effect conveyed to us of anything being yielded up or sacrificed. Nevertheless, there is a change, a change that makes us conscious that opposites have been reconciled, although the fugue marches to its close in indestructible might. This fugue is certainly, as Bekker has rightly insisted, the crown and *raison d'être* of the whole B flat major quartet. The other movements of the quartet, although it would be incorrect to say that they point towards the fugue, find their resolution within it. For these movements are, regarded separately, quite amazingly various, and they are quite unrelated to one another. There is, in fact, no reason why there should not have been more of them, or why their order should not have been different. For they merely depict various aspects of experience, all of which find their true relation, their reason for existence, in the light of the culminating experience of the fugue. In the first movement Beethoven chooses the sonata form, for he has to present to us a familiar contrast, the joy and energy of creation springing from a substratum of sorrow and suffering. This, to him, was one of life's dominant characteristics, but how lightly he touches on it! This movement has something of that note of reminiscence, of remoteness, that becomes so familiar to us in the last quartets. The wonderful little Presto that follows is a hint, although a pretty broad hint, of that delight in purely musical fantasy that must have been one of Beethoven's compensations. The content of the Andante is less obvious, but the complete absence here of all "great effects," the purely daylight atmosphere and the loving care with which all the details are treated, suggests that Beethoven is here concerned with the norm of human life, that priceless existence that even he could, at times, share, where there are no great passions, no ecstasies, and no profound despairs. It is an agreeably diversified life and certainly to be envied; its greatest contrasts are never violent. The *alla danza tedesca* movement, which smiles through tears, is deservedly popular for its haunting embodiment of a very general human experience, an experience that Beethoven evidently thought important, and which he expresses with the most exquisite and unforgettable charm. But the Cavatina has the profoundest emotional content of all these movements. We have already said that the quality of its yearning is yearning for the unattainable, for that close human intimacy, that love and sympathy, that Beethoven never experienced. There is nothing reminiscent about this movement. Its poignancy is of an experience altogether living. The preceding movements all have the delicacy of reminiscence; the Cavatina has the reality of a contemporary experience. This is an experience which is carried alive into the apotheosis of the fugue, and, transformed, helps to give it its note of heroic passion. The fugue was found too long and difficult by contemporary performers and audiences, as it has been until quite recently by most performers and audiences. As a result of the protests aroused by this movement, Beethoven substituted for it the present finale, the last complete composition that he wrote. Its effect is to make the whole quartet purely "human." Its reckless joy, rising at moments to the point of ecstasy, suggests no transcendental imaginings. It does not belong to the same region of consciousness as the fugue. If it be regarded as having any kinship with that experience and therefore as being in some sort a proper culmination of the quartet, it can only have the sort of kinship that exists between an emotion and the thought that provokes that emotion. This state of dithyrambic joy may, as it were, be the emotional reaction to, the generally understandable indication of, the state of illumination reached in the fugue, but it is no substitute for it. It has been suggested that Beethoven's unexpected docility in yielding to the request of his publisher to substitute the present finale for the fugue was due to irony, and some have read irony into this last movement. But to Beethoven an excellent reason for writing a new finale was that he would get a few more ducats for doing so, and as for its effect on the quartet, there are indications that Beethoven, at this time, paid little attention to contemporary opinion, but had much more confidence in posterity. He knew exactly what he had done in the original version of this quartet and he knew that the world would insist upon having it when it was ripe for it. In the meantime he bothered little about the lack of comprehension on the part of the musical amateurs of Vienna, and pocketed thankfully the extra ducats their insensibility brought him. For the rest he was willing to wait, for that his music would be a fructifying influence in a continually improving world he never had any doubt. Some years before he had written to a publisher, à propos of the Hammerclavier sonata, "Here is a sonata for you that will give the pianist something to do, and which will be played fifty years hence." He called it his greatest sonata, and he had spent immense pains on it. There is no question but that it existed in his mind as a perfectly organic unit. Yet at the same time he writes to Ries giving him *carte blanche* to leave out movements or to change their order if that will make the work more accessible to London audiences. That this indicates a certain lack of high expectations regarding the average "music lover" is pretty obvious but, considering that the quartet in B flat major is still never played in its original form, it is possible that he would have felt that very little higher demands could be made of that posterity he so much trusted.

The quartet in C sharp minor is the greatest of Beethoven's quartets, as he himself thought. It is also the most mystical of the quartets, and the one where the mystical vision is most perfectly sustained. It counts seven movements, but, regarded as an organic unity, it is the most complete of Beethoven's works. For the purposes of description, however, it is convenient to divide it into three parts. The opening fugue is the most superhuman piece of music that Beethoven has ever written. It is the completely unfaltering rendering into music of what we can only call the mystic vision. It has that serenity which, as Wagner said, speaking of these quartets, passes beyond beauty. Nowhere else in music are we made so aware, as here, of a state of consciousness surpassing our own, where our problems do not exist, and to which even our highest aspirations, those that we can formulate, provide no key. Those faint and troubling intimations we sometimes have of a vision different from and yet including our own, of a way of apprehending life, passionless, perfect and complete, that resolves all our discords, are here presented with the reality they had glimpsed. This impression of a superhuman knowledge, of a superhuman life being slowly frozen into shape, as it were, before our eyes, can be ambiguous. That passionless, remote calm can seem, as it did to Wagner, like a melancholy too profound for any tears. To Berlioz it was terrifying. To Beethoven himself it was the justification of, and the key to, life. In the light of this vision he surveys the world. That this vision was permanent with Beethoven is inconceivable. No men ever lived who could maintain such a state of illumination. This, we may be sure, is the last and greatest of Beethoven's spiritual discoveries, only to be grasped in the moments of his profoundest abstraction from the world. But it was sufficiently permanent to enable him to write the C sharp minor quartet in the light of it, a feat of concentration, of abstraction, of utter truthfulness, that is without equal. In the light of this experience we arrive, in the next movement, as a new-born creature in a new-born world. The virginal purity of this movement, its ethereal and crystalline quality, suggests to us a spirit not yet made flesh. After a brief introduction, which seems to usher in the act of incarnation, we find ourselves fully present in the warm, familiar human world. And yet how different it has become! The various aspects of experience that make up this human life, surveyed in the variations that follow, all have this different quality. They have the delicacy of shadows, but without their suggestion of impermanence. It is a transfigured world, where both our happiness and our prayers have become more pure and more simple. There is an indescribable lightness in this air; our bonds have become gossamer threads. And after floating through this outspread world we do, at that rapturous outbreak of trills in the last variation, rise up on wings and fly. And it is not only we, but all creation, that seems to be taking part in this exultant stirring. If ever a mystical vision of life has been presented in art it is here, in the sequence beginning with the fugue and ending with the last variation. It is this sequence, more than anything else in Beethoven's music, that convinces us that he had finally effected a synthesis of his whole experience. In these moments of illumination Beethoven had reached that state of consciousness that only the great mystics have ever reached, where there is no more discord. And in reaching it he retained the whole of his experience of life; he denied nothing. There follows an outbreak of the most exultant gaiety. There is no trace in the Scherzo of anything but the purest joy. Its most human quality is its humour, but humour so carefree and radiant is scarcely human. The adagio introduction to the finale has all the quality of a sorrowful awakening. It is as if the whole of the quartet preceding this movement had been a dream. But that, we are passionately convinced, cannot be true. The note of complete authenticity in that opening fugue cannot be mistaken. But it is certain that there is a withdrawal of the vision. It signifies, perhaps, a return from those heights on which no man may permanently live to this less real but more insistent world in which we are plunged in the last movement, a world where a heroism which is also pathetic marches to its end attended by yearning and pain. It may or it may not be of symbolic significance that Beethoven makes some use of the fugue theme in this last movement. But the character of the theme, as it occurs here, is entirely changed, and any symbolic significance it may have is not obvious.

Of the three great last quartets, the one in C sharp minor is the most unearthly and serene. The first of them, in A minor, is the least mystical and the one most full of human pain. It is, as a matter of historical fact, connected with a serious illness of Beethoven's and he himself wrote over the slow movement "Heiliger Dankgesang an die Gottheit eines Genesenen, in der lidischen Tonart." Acting on this hint the commentator A.-B. Marx sees in this quartet the description of a physical illness. This idea, as with so many apparently ridiculous "programmes" suggested by musical compositions, does, although inadequate, testify to certain genuine perceptions on the part of the commentator. The whole quartet may be taken as illustrating the normal aspect that life presented to the late Beethoven. Witness after witness testifies to the expression of profound sorrow that was habitual with him in the last years of his life, so that in mere contemplation of that dumb countenance the more emotional of them felt moved to tears. As we have said, we believe that in his most profound moments of insight and abstraction Beethoven was granted the solace of a more complete understanding. But such moments must have been comparatively rare, and could have occurred only in the midst of the artist's most profound isolation. We can well believe that no man ever saw the face of the transfigured Beethoven. But we believe that this man had suffered so greatly that the Beethoven men saw was the normal Beethoven of those days, poor, ill, stone-deaf, wretchedly housed, utterly alone, betrayed and abandoned by the one human being whose love he so desperately and pitifully craved. And from the depths of this man rose that solemn, pure and profound song of thanksgiving to the God-head. The yearning and the pain of the first movement (which ends, as only Beethoven would end, with what sounds like a startling and celestial trumpet call) is but little lightened in the second movement, where there reigns a spiritual weariness which is quite unmistakable. But again there comes that intimation of something celestial in an *alternativo* (that some writers find "curious" and others "humorous"!) where the first violin soars high over a pedal, and then comes the first moment of joy, real joy without any *arrière-pensé,* in the whole quartet. The first part is then repeated; the dominant mood is re-established. From this matrix rises the slow movement, the most heart-felt prayer from the most manly soul that has expressed itself in music. From this pure and sincere communion with his God there comes a quickened life, a rush of celestial joy, in the passage marked "Neue Kraft fühlend." The psychological resemblance between this transition and that in the second movement is obvious. Relief from pain, in this most pessimistic of Beethoven's quartets, comes only from above. Two main experiences form the texture of this quartet, exhaustion and defeat, and the new life bestowed as an act of grace from on high. With this "new strength" the next movement steps forth, but there is a wistfulness in its bravery. This is one of those movements, that occur only in the late Beethoven, where the very quality of the heroism reveals the heartache it is intended to conceal. This forlorn and lonely little march is marching to no victory. It is a gesture, brave but pathetic. With the *più allegro* section our forebodings are realized. Here is a shudder of realization, a resigned and hopeless cry, and we are again in the darkness of the struggle. Great waves of anguish seem to sweep over the struggling soul and at moments it seems that no resolution and faith can prevail against them. But a permanent strength, we may suppose, has come from those earlier celestial visions, from that pure and profound prayer, and the theme which before seemed to strive with difficulty against despair accelerates, until, in the final Presto, it rings out victoriously, but victor in a victory so hard-won that we are left with none of that feeling of exultant triumph with which we have watched so many of Beethoven's victories, but rather with a feeling of slightly incredulous relief, of thankfulness still tinged with doubt.

CHAPTER TEN

The Final Stage

THERE SEEMS to be no reason to doubt that the great bulk of Beethoven's work is of permanent value. The greatest function of a work of art is to present us with a higher organization of experience. It is on this that its claim to "greatness" depends. It does not seem that the "greatness" and the "beauty" of a work of art are identical. What constitutes the beauty of a work of art is a hitherto unresolved problem with which, in this book, we are not concerned. That Beethoven's music is more beautiful than any other music we are not inclined to assert; that it is greater than any other music has been, on the whole, the general opinion ever since it appeared. Its greatness depends on what we have called its spiritual content, and this is something that the listener perceives directly, although he may be entirely unable to formulate it. Beethoven's work will live because of the permanent value, to the human race, of the experiences it communicates. These experiences are valuable because they are in the line of human development; they are experiences to which the race, in its evolutionary march, aspires. At a given period certain experiences may be current, and may be given popular artistic expression, which are not valuable. In our own day, for example, a certain nervous excitability and spiritual weariness, due to specific and essentially temporary causes, has informed a good deal of contemporary art. Small artists can flourish in an age which is not fit for heroes to live in. But such manifestations are of quite local importance. The great artist achieves a relative immortality because the experiences he deals with are as fundamental for humanity as are hunger, sex, and the succession of day and night. It does not follow that the experiences he communicates are elementary. They may belong to an order of consciousness that very few men have attained but, in that case, they must be in the line of human development; we must feel them as prophetic. Beethoven's late music communicates experiences that very few people can normally possess. But we value these experiences because we feel they are not freakish. They correspond to a spiritual synthesis which the race has not achieved but which, we may suppose, it is on the way to achieving. It is only the very greatest kind of artist who presents us with experiences that we recognize both as fundamental and as in advance of anything we have hitherto known. With such art we make contact, for a moment, with

> The prophetic soul of the wide world
> Dreaming on things to come.

It is to this kind of art that Beethoven's greatest music belongs and it is, perhaps, the greatest in that kind.

In Beethoven's earlier work we are dealing, for the most part, with experiences which are not only fundamental but universal. This is what is meant by some writers when they call this music more "objective" than his later work. The spiritual content of the most characteristic of Beethoven's "second period" work may be summed up as achievement through heroism in spite of suffering. This music is probably still what the bulk of listeners mean when they speak of Beethoven. To the majority of people suffering is still one of life's major characteristics, and it is that characteristic, more than any other, that determines our attitude towards life. The spiritual essence of life, as presented by Beethoven is, we feel, consistent with our deepest experiences, and the solution he presents is one consistent with our loftiest aspirations. This music has the note of authenticity. Its sorrow is real, and so is its heroism. The passionate reverence that so many thousands have felt for the author of this music (a phenomenon quite without parallel in the case of any other musician) is a testimony to the profundity, universality and genuineness of the experiences it communicates. No artist, more than Beethoven, has dealt with the things that most deeply concern mankind. And we can be encouraged and made hopeful by the solution he presents because he convinces us that he knows, in all their bitterness, the elements of the problem. What optimism this man preaches has, we feel, been earned. This attitude towards Beethoven is, and always has been, very general and, except on the basis of quite arbitrary theories about the meaninglessness of music, is perfectly justified. Beethoven could compose music "for the fun of it," but in all his greatest work he was concerned to make explicit, through the medium of his art, states of consciousness evoked by his profoundest experiences. For his ability to use his medium he would have to be ranked amongst the greatest composers; for the quality of what he expressed he is beyond comparison.

In Beethoven's personal history the attitude towards life characteristic of his "second period" was found to be insufficient. It is true that abandonment of the struggle, as preached by such a man as Schopenhauer, was never accepted by Beethoven. But it seems likely that he passed through a period when his resistance and endurance were attended by no hope. The fugue of the Hammerclavier sonata is informed with a most furious energy, but he would be a strange listener who should be inspired by it to anything that could be called courageous optimism. But in the ninth symphony we are aware that, although all the elements of the old problem are present, something new is being said. A synthesis has been achieved. Suffering no longer plays the part it did in the attitude of the young Beethoven. In listening to this symphony, and particularly its first and third movements, we have the feeling we have only with Beethoven's late music, that something hitherto unknown and yet that passionately matters to us, is being revealed. A new kind of awareness is communicated to us. No elements of our experience are omitted, but the light in which they are presented transforms them. And in the last quartets it appears that quite new elements enter.

The opening movement of the C sharp minor quartet seems to reveal an unsuspected possibility of the mind, to communicate to us a state of consciousness hardly analogous to anything we have previously experienced. Even the world of the ninth symphony contains nothing that so far surpasses the norm of human experience. Perhaps the only thing in Beethoven's music that would serve as a bridge to that unearthly experience is the last movement of the last pianoforte sonata. That great flight ends, we may suppose, on the threshold of the region from which the fugue proceeds.

It so happens that Beethoven's last complete work, the quartet in F major, Op. 135, makes a fitting end to his great series of explorations. It is the work of a man who is fundamentally at peace. It is the peace of a man who has known conflict, but whose conflicts are now reminiscent. This quality is most apparent in the last movement, with its motto "Muss es sein? Es muss sein!" According to Schindler this motto had its origin in a joke but, as used here, it is a summary of the great Beethovenian problem of destiny and submission. But Beethoven had found his solution of that problem, and he treats the old question here with the lightness, even the humour, of one to whom the issue is settled and familiar. There is no real conflict depicted in this last movement; the portentous question meets with a jovial, almost exultant answer, and the ending is one of perfect confidence. The question raised here is, indeed, seen in the light of the profound peace which dominates the slow movement of this quartet. If we may judge from this quartet, and also from Beethoven's actual last composition, the present finale of the B flat quartet, it would appear that at the end of his life the inner Beethoven, the Beethoven who expressed himself in music, was content.

The quartet in F, Op. 135, was finished at Gneixendorf ("the name sounds like the breaking of an axletree," said Beethoven), where Beethoven was staying during the late autumn of 1826 with his nephew in the house of his brother Johann. The purpose of this visit was to find a suitable asylum for the young man, who had recently left hospital after his attempt at suicide, until the time elapsed when he was due to join the army. The visit was not a success. Beethoven was morose and his nephew was irked by the restraints imposed upon him. From what we know of this visit it again becomes clear that Beethoven's music, at this time, proceeded in entire independence of the contemporary circumstances of his life. On December 2, Beethoven and his nephew returned to Vienna. Owing to exposure on the journey Beethoven arrived ill. A complication of diseases, amongst them dropsy, rapidly developed. The sick-room was appallingly dirty and uncared for, and the medical attention not very efficient. Beethoven was four times operated on for dropsy and then abandoned hope. Except for the bank shares, destined for his nephew, and which he therefore resolutely refused to sell, he had very little money. He appealed for assistance to friends in England, and the Philharmonic Society responded by sending him one hundred pounds, a gift for which he was extremely grateful, but which he never lived to touch. Some of it was used afterwards to pay his funeral expenses. Otherwise, according to Schindler, he could not have been decently buried without selling one of the bank shares. During his illness Beethoven passed much of his time in reading Handel, whose complete works had been presented to him by Stumpff. He had a special liking for this composer. Indeed, he had said more than once that he placed Handel above all others. A reference to this reading, which also throws light on the attitude in which Beethoven awaited death, occurs in a letter by his physician, Dr. Wawruch, written after the fourth operation for dropsy.

> "No words of comfort could brace him up, and when I promised him alleviation of his sufferings with the coming of the vitalizing weather of spring he answered with a smile, 'My day's work is finished. If there were a physician could help me his name should be called Wonderful.' This pathetic allusion to Handel's 'Messiah' touched me so deeply that I had to confess its correctness to myself with profound emotion."

The end came some time after five o'clock on the afternoon of March 26, 1827. Beethoven had been unconscious for two days, and his death struggles were violent. His last moments are described by Hüttenbrenner, who, with Beethoven's sister-in-law, made one of the only two people present at the end. There had been a violent storm, and suddenly there was a lightning flash and a great crash of thunder. It seems to have aroused the dying man from his unconsciousness. He raised his clenched fist, opened his eyes and looked upwards for several seconds with a "very serious, threatening expression." As the hand dropped he fell back dead.

In this sketch of Beethoven's spiritual development

we have regarded him chiefly as an explorer. What we may call his emotional nature was sensitive, discriminating, and profound, and his circumstances brought him an intimate acquaintance with the chief characteristics of life. His realization of the character of life was not hindered by insensitiveness, as was Wagner's, nor by religion, as was Bach's. There was nothing in this man, either natural or acquired, to blunt his perceptions. And he was not merely sensitive; he was not merely a reflecting mirror. His experiences took root and grew. An inner life of quite extraordinary intensity was in process of development till the very end. Other artists, of those few whose spirits were both sensitive and free, seem to have passed through similar stages of development. But perhaps even Shakespeare never reached that final stage of illumination that is expressed in some of Beethoven's late music. The other steps of the journey he knew, but Shakespeare never wrote his C sharp minor quartet. It is possible, indeed, that Beethoven's late music is unique, not only in music, but in the whole of art.

Although we have regarded Beethoven's music from its philosophic aspect, it is not for the purpose of deducing a philosophy from it. Beethoven's greatest music has meaning in the sense that it is not a mere pattern of sounds, but possesses a spiritual content; nevertheless, it does not in any sense express a philosophy. It expresses certain primary experiences as organized in the mind of this particular artist. But this organization of experience is utterly different from the organization of experience presented in a philosophy. It is an organization to which the criteria of logical coherence do not in the least apply. Beethoven's profoundest attitude towards life, as expressed in his music, owes nothing to the mediation of his intelligence. The synthesis of his experience that is achieved by a great artist proceeds according to laws of which we know almost nothing, but purely intellectual formulation plays a very small part in it. If Beethoven reached the state, as we believe he did, where he achieved the "submission" he felt to be so necessary, it was not through any process of reasoning. And his realization of the necessity of submission could not have been reached by any such process. As a crude analogy we may suggest that there are spiritual appetites, as there are bodily ones, necessary for development but which, like the sexual appetite, make their appearance only at a certain stage of growth. Comparatively few men, even amongst artists, manifest a true spiritual growth. Their attitude towards life is relatively fixed; it may be exemplified with more richness and subtlety as they mature, but it does not develop. Such a transition, as we find from Beethoven's "second" to his "third" period, where nothing is abandoned and yet where everything is changed, is extremely rare. Beethoven, therefore, although he preached no philosophy, is of philosophical importance because he adds one to the very few cases that exist of a genuine spiritual development. Such cases, it might be said, do nothing to help the development of mankind. Beethoven's music illustrates the development, but throws no light on the process by which it came about. But such revelations have a strangely haunting quality. We may be unable to earn for ourselves the capacity to utter the prayer of thanksgiving of the A minor quartet, or to reach the state of final serenity of the fugue of the C sharp minor quartet, but we can henceforth take but little account of attitudes towards life that leave no room for these experiences, attitudes which deny them or explain them away. And our conviction that these experiences are valuable, even to us, is reinforced by the whole bulk of Beethoven's work. If they stood alone these superhuman utterances might seem to us those of an oracle who was hardly a man. But we know, from the rest of his music, that Beethoven was a man who experienced all that we can experience, who suffered all that we can suffer. If, in the end, he seems to reach a state "above the battle" we also know that no man ever knew more bitterly what the battle is.

John William Navin Sullivan, the son of a poor Irish sailor, was born in 1886; he died in 1937 in England. Educated at University College, London, he was a mathematician, philosopher of science, reviewer for *The Times* (London), and an amateur pianist. Among his numerous publications are *Aspects of Science* (1922), *History of Mathematics in Europe* (1925), *Three Men Discuss Relativity* (1926), *Present Day Astronomy* (1930), and *Science: A New Outlook* (1935). Mr. Sullivan's *Beethoven* was originally published in 1927.

This Book is set in *Granjon,* a type named in compliment to Robert Granjon, type-cutter and printer—Antwerp, Lyons, Paris—active from 1523 to 1590. The boldest and most original designer of his time, he was one of the first to practice the trade of type-founder apart from that of printer. Composed, printed, and bound by The Colonial Press, Inc., Clinton, Massachusetts. Paper manufactured by S. D. Warren Company, Boston. Cover design by Leo Lionni.

V-131	Thackeray, W. M.	VANITY FAIR
V-713	Tolstoy, Leo	THE KREUTZER SONATA
V-154	Tracy, Honor	STRAIGHT AND NARROW PATH
V-202	Turgenev, Ivan	TORRENTS OF SPRING
V-711	Turgenev, Ivan	THE VINTAGE TURGENEV Volume I: SMOKE, FATHERS AND SONS, FIRST LOVE
V-712	Turgenev, Ivan	Volume II: ON THE EVE, RUDIN, A QUIET SPOT, DIARY OF A SUPERFLUOUS MAN
V-152	Waugh, Evelyn	THE LOVED ONE

VINTAGE BELLES-LETTRES

V-708	Aksakov, Sergey	YEARS OF CHILDHOOD
V-22	Barzun, Jacques	THE ENERGIES OF ART
V-191	Beer, Thomas	THE MAUVE DECADE
V-80	Beerbohm, Max	SEVEN MEN *and* TWO OTHERS
V-75	Camus, Albert	THE MYTH OF SISYPHUS *and* Other Essays
V-30	Camus, Albert	THE REBEL
V-216	Chamberlain, N. (ed.)	A VINTAGE FOOD SAMPLER
V-64	Evans, Bergen	THE NATURAL HISTORY OF NONSENSE
V-112	Gide, André	JOURNALS, Volume I: 1889-1924
V-113	Gide, André	JOURNALS, Volume II: 1924-1949
V-104	Huxley, Aldous	BEYOND THE MEXIQUE BAY
V-41	James, Henry	THE FUTURE OF THE NOVEL
V-235	Kaplan, Abraham	THE NEW WORLD OF PHILOSOPHY
V-167	La Rochefoucauld	MAXIMS
V-230	Leedom, William	THE VINTAGE WINE BOOK
V-193	Malraux, André	TEMPTATION OF THE WEST
V-55	Mann, Thomas	ESSAYS
V-232	Mencken, H. L.	TREATISE ON THE GODS
V-34	Montaigne, Michel de	AUTOBIOGRAPHY
V-197	Morgan, F. (ed.)	HUDSON REVIEW ANTHOLOGY
V-54	Nicolson, Harold	SOME PEOPLE
V-24	Ransom, John Crowe	POEMS AND ESSAYS
V-85	Stevens, Wallace	POEMS
V-53	Synge, J. M.	THE ARAN ISLANDS *and* Other Writings
V-194	Valéry, Paul	THE ART OF POETRY

VINTAGE BIOGRAPHY AND AUTOBIOGRAPHY